Contents

Preface

Nearly ten years has passed since the manuscript for the first edition of *Business Ethics* was sent to Prentice Hall. The passage of time has taken its toll. Some issues that seemed important then are no longer in the forefront of public debate. New issues have arisen to take their place. A new edition was required.

As I thought about writing a new edition, it occurred to me that a second edition might be stronger if I had a trusted friend and business ethics scholar rewrite the first edition as a starting point for the second. It also seemed that a second edition might benefit from a philosophical perspective somewhat different from my own. Ron Duska of Rosemont College agreed to perform these tasks and to be the co-author of the second edition. His interests in both Aristotle and communitarian theory are reflected in this edition.

This edition begins much like the first edition—from the perspective of a new employee as he or she assumes the first job. We try to show how moral obligations arise when one accepts a position with a firm, for example, an obligation to be loyal. Some of these job-related obligations help us to escape from some nasty moral dilemmas. On the other hand, some of the obligations that an employer or supervisor may try to impose on an employee are illegitimate. We argue that some criteria are needed to sort out the legitimate from the illegitimate in these cases.

One means for distinguishing legitimate from illegitimate job-related concerns is to determine what constitutes a morally appropriate theory of the purpose of a business firm. In Chapter 2, several models are evaluated critically. Yet another means for distinguishing legitimate from illegitimate job-related obligations is to see if these obligations are consistent with universal moral norms that underlie all moral institutions including business. Chapter 3 addresses this issue from a Kantian perspective. Chapter 3 also provides a morally acceptable standard for distinguishing legitimate from illegitimate moral demands on corporate conduct. We conclude that business firms have an obligation to avoid harm and a somewhat weaker obligation to *prevent* harm. Business firms do not have an obligation to do good. These first three chapters provide a theoretical structure for business ethics. Chapter 4 uses standard stakeholder analysis. In that chapter we analyze a manager's obligation to stockholders, employees, customers, and the community. Discussions of drug testing and product liability are new to this edition.

Having established a theory of business ethics, we then ask how that theory can be put into practice. Chapter 5 considers the strengths and weaknesses of both self-regulation and government regulation. We conclude in Chapter 6 by addressing the question of why a business firm or business person should do what is morally appropriate when they can get away with doing something that is not moral.

Readers familiar with business will recognize many of the issues discussed within the chapter—deceptive advertising, loyalty to the firm versus whistle blowing, stockholder interests, the profit motive, and equal opportunity. Readers familiar with philosophy will be familiar with many theories—Kantianism, utilitarianism, Aristotelianism, Rawlsianism—and with many of the issues—equal opportunity versus equal results, the problem of why we should be moral, weakness of will, the scope of human rights, competing theories of freedom, and the limits of law. It is our hope that readers from both perspectives will come away from this book with a deeper appreciation and understanding of the central issues that are referred to as business ethics.

The book, however, does not provide a handbook for settling all ethical issues that arise in business. There is no such handbook for business or, as a matter of fact, for any other area of ethics. The book does describe how a person can take the ethical point of view in business and provides some tools for implementing ethical decisions in business. We think that is all a book in business ethics can do, but we think that a book that does those things is of value.

The manuscript benefitted from much criticism—both friendly and hostile. We deeply appreciate the careful comments provided by the general editors of the series, John Atwell and Elizabeth Beardsley. We also express our thanks to the anonymous Prentice Hall reviewers. Ron Duska extends gratitude to the Pew Memorial Trust for a grant that provided release time for writing this book. This book would not have been completed without the loyal, unstinting assistance of Sandy Manno who provided the secretarial support services.

Chapter One

My Position and Its Duties

Suppose that your first job after college involves a position in the purchasing department of a medium-sized manufacturing plant. You are hired to obtain about six products, all of which are essential to the electric clocks that your firm manufactures. You report to a Mr. Norwood, who has worked with this firm for ten years. Your assignment, which was detailed in the job description and in subsequent interviews, was to negotiate the best contract you could for the six products under your control. You were told specifically that it is the policy of your company *not* to give special consideration to those firms that had been awarded contracts in the past. With this information clearly in mind, you begin negotiations for a contract for the ensuing year.

One day Mr. Norwood and a sales representative from the Slow Spring Company take you to lunch. Both persons make it clear to you that Slow Spring is to get the bid. In return, you will get a kickback of $10,000 and Mr. Norwood will get a kickback of $5,000. Mr. Norwood indicates that failure to cooperate will result in bad evaluations and eventual dismissal. Indeed, Mr. Norwood has a file on the person who held your job previously. It contains a set of bad evaluations and a dismissal notice. You consider informing Mr. Norwood's supervisors. Discrete inquiry, however, indicates that Mr. Norwood's supervisor is busy covering up some design flaws in the clock—a decision dictated by top management on the basis that it will be cheaper to suffer a few consumer complaints than to correct the problem—at least for this model year.

This is your first job and good jobs are hard to find. What should you do? You face an ethical dilemma.

THE STOCK SALE

You are a stockbroker for a small firm, Valley Securities, which is part of a syndicate that sells new offerings for a large underwriting firm, Acme Underwriters. Your firm's relationship with Acme is crucial for its financial stability.

1

Acme releases a stock issue that your own analysts indicate is not very good. Your boss would like to see the issue pushed in spite of its shakiness in order to mollify Acme, but he won't push you to unload it on your clients. What should you do?

A colleague of yours, in spite of the analyst's report, pushes the stock on some of his customers, thus making a bonus for himself and pleasing the boss. Two weeks later, he takes the analyst's report, changes the date, and sends it out to his clients, who have just purchased the stock, and convinces them to sell it. Thus, he doubles his commission. You are aware of this. What should you do? Should you report him? To whom? Why?

This is another ethical dilemma.

THE ORGANIZATION OF THIS BOOK

This book on business ethics will not provide clear-cut answers to the dilemmas just described. Usually there are no clear-cut definitive answers to moral dilemmas. It may be clear that one shouldn't take kickbacks, but is it clear that one shouldn't take a kickback if not taking it puts one's job in jeopardy? It may be clear that in the best of all possible worlds one should report improper behavior, but what is the point if the manager whom one is to report the behavior to is also engaged in improper behavior or at least winks at improper behavior? It may be clear that falsifying stock reports is improper, but is it clear that you should report one's colleague's improper behavior? This book will provide a set of theoretical tools that can help you face dilemmas intelligently, prevent them if you are in a position to do so, or work them out as much as possible. The book will not only help make you sensitive to the existence of the ethical dimension that necessarily pervades the world of business but also help make you capable of recognizing ethical issues when they arise.

One of the assumptions of this book is that ethical decisions in business are similar to other business decisions in their complexity and open-endedness. In marketing or personnel management, for example, one needs to identify precisely the variables that make up the problem; to decide on an acceptable solution by looking at various elements such as costs, benefits, legalities, and contractual commitments, not to mention feasibility and desirability; and to act so that the solution is achieved or a course of action is initiated as quickly and efficiently as possible. Consider the decision a cereal company makes as to whether it should introduce a new product—Crazy Stars. The company will perform a market analysis of all the target populations, plus consider start-up costs, the extent of risk, the future economic outlook, and other factors in making the decision whether to introduce Crazy Stars. Both the complexity and the open-endedness of a decision regarding an ethical problem—for example, should a company fire a long-standing loyal employee whose sales are slipping, or should a subordinate report his boss for taking kickbacks—are similar to that involved in deciding whether to introduce a new cereal. However, rather than appealing to feasibility studies and doing cost-benefit analyses in order to decide, one appeals to ethical theories. The intention of this book is to have the reader appreciate what these ethical theories are and how they can be used to help make decisions about the problems of ethics that arise within business. The book will show how a rational attempt to solve these problems requires a consideration and use of some of the principles of ethical theory. But what exactly is ethics and ethical theory?

The word *ethics* refers to many things: a code of rules, a set of principles one lives by, or the study of what is right or wrong. We will begin with the latter. Simply put, ethics, for our purposes, is a study that attempts to shed light on the question "What should one do?" Thus, the focus of ethics is on human actions or behavior.

But it doesn't concentrate on all human actions or behavior. First, it focuses on that behavior which is deliberate or free, since it is silly to say I should do something if I am not free to do otherwise. Second, it focuses on behavior that affects me and others, but in a serious way. For example, slurping my soup and not putting oil in my car are deliberate actions, and they are actions that *should or should not* be done, for they are actions that affect me or others. But they are not ethical matters, the subject of ethical consideration, because they do not affect us in a serious way.

In evaluating such behavior, ethics appeals to reasons to justify or condemn it. For example, if I promise to lend my son a car and then change my mind, he is entitled to ask me why I am not keeping my promise. The question asks for a *reason* to *justify* my action. Most of us would agree that promises should be kept. Thus, "promises should be kept" can be seen as an ethical rule we think we should follow. Call it a rule of common morality. If we decide not to obey that rule, if we think we *should* not or need not follow it, then we need to *justify* our proposed behavior with a "good reason." For instance, if I tell my son he cannot have the car *because* the brake line is leaking oil, I have given a good reason for breaking my promise. If, on the other hand, I say to my son, "You can't have the car because it is mine and I just don't feel like giving it to you, and to heck with my promise," that is assuredly not a good reason, and my behavior is not justified. In short, I *shouldn't* do that.

DOING ONE'S JOB

If we look at business and ask "What should one do?" perhaps the most obvious answer, the simplest rule, is the following: "One should do one's job." Here we have a straightforward rule that common morality gives us. Of course, one could in a sort of perverse way, ask, "Why should one do one's job?" but that would be a question asking for a higher principle of justification. But even that doesn't seem too difficult. We could say that it seems fairly obvious that anyone who freely agrees (makes some sort of contract or promise) to take on a job also agrees to meet the responsibilities of that job. For reasons we will discuss later, that puts the individual under a moral requirement to do one's job. You should do your job, because it is a responsibility freely taken on and "One should meet one's responsibilities," or you signed a contract and "One should abide by one's contracts," or you made a promise and "One should keep one's promises." All of these, then, provide reasons for the rule "One should do one's job." Let's examine what that rule entails.

Within business, every person has a position, a job to perform—assembly-line worker, salesperson, accountant, public relations specialist, chief executive, member of the governing board. This position is defined by a set of rules or practices that indicate what that person should do; that is, what that person is expected to do, what *obligations* or *duties* that person has, or, more commonly, what *responsibilities* that person has. In some cases there is a detailed formal job description along with an employees' handbook specifying precisely what the person is to do. In other cases, there are just vague prescriptions of what to do and few if any formal rules or requirements. Indeed, in some cases people get to define their job as they go along. Their responsibility is as general as to find out what the company needs and do it or get it done. Finally, there are the customary expectations that go along with the job—those of society and one's fellow workers. It seems clear then that there are ethical and moral responsibilities in the field of business ethics, beginning with the responsibility to do one's job.

To insist one should do one's job is to adopt a "role morality." To develop this point we will compare a job to a role so that, in a sense, to take on a job is to take on a role. According to Dorothy Emmet

> The concept of a role is...needed in describing the repeatable patterns of social relations which are not mere physical facts and which are structured partly by the rules of acceptable behavior in the society in question.[1]

If we use this concept of a role, we see how much a job is a role. The society in question here would be the business or company. The company has patterns of social relations that structure the relations of the people in the firm and give those people their own rules of acceptable behavior. Thus, a chief executive officer (CEO), a manager, as well as an assembly-line worker—all have roles to follow.

All of these "roles," according to philosopher R.S. Downie, are "...a cluster of rights and duties with some sort of social function."[2] The role (job) then has rights and duties that constitute rules to be followed in order to fulfill the social function of the company.

These roles contain legal, customary, and moral elements. Some of the legal elements are contractual. The contractual elements are explicit formal rules and regulations included in the contracts and handbooks that serve as the job description or the job responsibilities that one must follow if one is to do one's job "properly." Those contractual elements obviously have a legal dimension to the extent that failure to honor one's contract will provide legal grounds for dismissal. But there are other legal elements besides that. There are those involving governmental standards whereby government regulatory agencies require certain behaviors of companies and their agents. Further, legal elements surrounding a job include the number of hours one is to work, the starting and quitting times, and, most important, the goal or goals that one is to accomplish. Within unionized industries, these legal elements are spelled out in the collective bargaining agreement. For instance, in an automobile assembly plant, a worker will be paid a certain number of dollars per hour for 40 hours of work per week to attach doors to auto bodies where the assembly line is to operate at 20 finished automobiles per hour.

But the job description is not exhausted by its legal elements. A new person on the assembly line quickly learns that there are customs governing both how one does the job and how one interacts with colleagues. The new employee learns the "etiquette" surrounding a job. Failure to follow job etiquette does not provide legitimate grounds for dismissal, but violating it can make one's relations with one's colleagues unpleasant. If the violations of job etiquette are serious enough, one's colleagues will find ways to drive the new employee out or get the person fired. Someone entering the job market should not underestimate the constraints that job etiquette puts on individual behavior. Sometimes the customary elements surrounding a job provide more constraints than do the legal elements.

It is obvious from the foregoing remarks that following the legal rules and conforming to job etiquette is in one's self-interest. Behavior in one's self-interest is often called "prudent" behavior, and for many persons "To do what's good for me" seems a sufficient answer to the question "What should one do?" But very often we have responsibilities and duties that require behavior at odds with self-interest. Often, what we call duties are precisely those actions that should be done even when they are not in one's interest. I may have had a late night and want to sluff off on my job, but my duty or responsibility to do my job requires me to go to work in spite of what I feel like doing. It is precisely where self-interest conflicts with my duties to others that we most clearly enter the domain of ethics. Moral injunctions do not appeal to self-interest but rather to the moral notion of duty or responsibility. Suppose that one could get away with not doing one's job very well or with not being respectful to one's colleagues. Moreover, suppose that it is in one's self-interest to avoid such responsibilities when one could get away with it. Self-interest would allow it; ethical considerations would not. Morality requires that you do your job well, or at least to a preestablished level of acceptability, and respect your colleagues and promises, even when you could get away with not doing it.

It is important to note that some rules have both a moral and a legal component to them. For example, the common law of agency[3] requires that an employee (the agent) has duties of loyalty, obedience, and confidentiality to the employer (the principal). This common law tradition has been formalized in Sections 383 and 385 of the Restatement of Agency (revised in 1958). These employee duties of loyalty, obedience, and confidentiality will be discussed later.

As another example, consider the job of an accountant. Accountants have both a legal and moral responsibility to protect private information about their clients. More generally, the responsibility to abide by one's contract is both legal, because the law requires persons to honor their contracts, and moral, because of the moral obligations to keep one's promises.

In summary, to take on a job is to enter into a social institution or practice that has a set of rules and to voluntarily submit to those rules. These rules constitute a series of norms for adequate performance. Perhaps an analogy with parenthood would make these points clearer. One is designated a "parent," assumes the role of a parent, either by being the mother or father of a child or by adopting a child. Being a parent brings with it obligations and responsibilities. How good a parent one is can be determined by judging how well one performs in carrying out those obligations and responsibilities. Some parents are better than others. The extensive and willful neglect of one's parental responsibilities is universally branded as immoral. Another way of saying this, as the philosopher F.H. Bradley does, is to say that being a parent involves having a certain "station in life," and with that "station" comes certain "duties."[4] As it is with parenthood, so also it is with one's job. "Once one has assumed the role, it binds with obligations of right and wrong."[5] In other words, a job can be viewed as a "station in life" and it has its duties just as parenthood has. Thus, people have obligations as a part of their job, and what people ought to do depends in part on the jobs they have.

IMPLICATIONS

If the role relation of the employer and employee is moral, then it is more than economic where an economic relation is defined as an equilibrium of competing self-interests between the employer and the employee. Consider an assembly-line worker who is receiving a weekly wage of $400 for 40 hours of piecework. If the relation of the assembly-line worker to his or her employer is simply economic, what incentive does the worker have for quality control? The worker would like high compensation for relatively few hours of work. The employer would prefer low compensation. Each is well aware of the attitude of the other. In such a situation, the worker would consider the job as simply a job. The worker would view it with indifference or even hostility; the temptation would be to do as little as possible. Inevitably this attitude would have bad effects either on the products produced or on interpersonal relationships where the person holding the job interacts with the public.

What is needed in addition to a wage is a job that is "rewarding." Jobs done for purely economic reasons are alienating and not self-satisfying. They depress workers' morale, and they make workers feel like machines. Hannah Arendt distinguished between "labor" and "work."[6] Labor is the type of job that one does over and over, like sweeping a floor, that doesn't lead to any discernible results that last. This type of job is generally looked upon as meaningless. The more meaningful jobs result in a product that lasts, or a service that makes a significant difference in someone's life. Here craftsmanship becomes important and workers can take "pride in their work." But the harsh economic realities often mitigate against that; sometimes competition requires lesser quality and someone has to perform the menial tasks. When competition requires a compromise on quality, workers are torn between their responsibility to their "work" or "craft" and their responsibility to their employer. And if dirty work has to be done, are there additional responsibilities on the employer to those who do the menial "dirty" work? These are not easy issues to resolve, but they do involve the moral element.

If one recognizes that any job brings with it a set of responsibilities and duties on the part of worker and employer, and if one adopts the moral point of view, then a job can never be viewed simply as a job. Economic bargaining certainly remains important, but we can argue that the employee has not just a duty to do the job but to do the job "well," and the employer has a duty not merely to provide minimum compensation but a "fair" salary and safe, pleasant working conditions.

The concern with service and quality, doing one's job well—that is, beyond minimal contractual economic conditions and expectations—is most explicit in those jobs we call professions. Dorothy Emmet describes a profession as follows:

> A profession...carries with it the notion of a standard of performance, it is not only a way of making a living, but one in which the practitioners have a fiduciary trust to maintain certain standards. These are partly standards of competence, or technical ability in carrying out functions valued in the society. But not only so: professional competence has to be joined with professional integrity....A professional man carries out his functions in relation to people who also stand in a particular role relation to him. The relationship carries specific obligations, to be distinguished from those of purely personal morality, or from general obligations to human beings as such.[7]

The more professional a job, the "weightier" the responsibilities that go with it. The Harvard Business School has as its motto—"To Make Business a Profession." In committing itself to that motto, the Harvard Business School commits itself to educating persons entering business in the obligations and responsibilities of a profession, educating them into the fiduciary standards required by a professional approach.

But why do weightier obligations fall on professionals? Some suggest that the practitioner of a profession exercises a special technical skill on behalf of a client—a skill that the client needs but does not possess. Traditionally, the professional skill is a service skill, specifically a skill that benefits humankind through giving of service. Here the agent, the doctor, lawyer, or teacher, is committed to helping the principal, the person being served. Consequently, the primary goal of such a skill is altruistic. The professional's function is to meet the needs of the principal. Reimbursement for such skills is secondary. Thus, to exercise a skill for the benefit of others places the professional person in a special moral relation with his or her clients. After all, if it is morally praiseworthy to serve others, and one's job is to serve others, then failure to perform one's professional role diminishes one's claim to the respect and praise that attend the practice of the profession. Finally, as Emmet notes, a profession carries its own notion of standards of performance to be met. Practitioners have a "fiduciary" trust to maintain those standards.

Professionals are not alone in having a moral obligation to do their job well. Almost every job has an impact on other people. The auto assembly-line worker who places the door on its hinges is in a moral relationship with those who purchase the company's line of cars. The person who purchases the car assumes that the doors were attached with care. Carelessly hanging a door that comes detached from the auto body, thus resulting in injury to the occupant, is an action capable of being evaluated morally. The careless person has committed a morally blameworthy act because people get harmed. If shoddy work can injure the unwary purchaser of a product, there is an obvious moral responsibility to avoid shoddy work, because we are morally obliged to avoid doing that which can harm others.

But what about garbage collectors and busboys? Careless performance on their part is usually not dangerous, although careless performance may be messy. Even here it can be argued that there are moral obligations associated with the jobs—albeit of a much more minor nature. First, garbage collectors are being paid by society for a service, and that puts contractual and promissory obligations on them. Morally, they have agreed to perform a service and therefore are morally obligated to perform an honest day's work for an honest day's pay. Moreover, to cause annoyance and inconvenience needlessly is morally blameworthy, and in the case of the busboy, his shoddy performance harms the restaurant owner.

Thus, nearly every job places you in morally relevant relations with other people. Both the extent and the stringency of the moral responsibilities associated with your job depend on the type of job that you have—very stringent for those whose work or service impacts on people in serious ways, such as doctors, air-traffic controllers, etc., and much less stringent on those whose jobs don't have as much impact, such as garbage collectors and busboys.

We can say, then, that each job carries with it a responsibility or obligation to do what the job or role demands. This is because there is either an explicit contract with a very complete description of the job and its obligations, or there is a less formal agreement, where the agent or the employee agrees to do what is in the best interest of the principal. Whether the description should be spelled out or not depends very much on circumstances. Sometimes specificity is required and sometimes not. For example, you don't have to tell a cleaning-service person to dust under radiators, or carpenters to use strong enough beams in construction. On the other hand, far too often disputes about job performance arise as a result of misunderstandings and misinformation about job expectations and methods of evaluation. Often, young women were placed in "management training positions" where the first and last tasks assigned were clerical and secretarial. That's where their management training ended. There is a customary expectation that management training means just that—*management* training. Precise job descriptions that are accessible publicly might help prospective employees to make vocational choices more accurately. This is particularly helpful when old customs are being challenged. For example, some secretaries have justified not making coffee because such chores do not fall within a secretary's job description. At any rate, where the job description and expectations are fully spelled out, ambiguity about one's responsibilities can be reduced.

Another implication of approaching business ethics by analyzing the obligations that accompany an employee's job is that it frequently provides an excellent framework for the resolution of certain problems in business ethics. Consider the following two cases.[8]

THE ENGINEERING CONSULTANT

You are an engineering consultant to mining firms. Surestrike Mining hires you to evaluate one of its producing mines. You do so and discover that the mine has moved under adjacent property owned by West Virginia Mining Co. Hence, Surestrike does not have mineral rights to the coal being mined.

You report to Surestrike that it is infringing on the mineral rights of West Virginia Mining. Management thanks you and pays you. Six months later you discover that Surestrike is still mining under that property and that it has not notified West Virginia Mining of your findings. Your contract with Surestrike provided that you would not disclose any findings to a third party. What should you do?

WHISTLE-BLOWING—ALPHA CORPORATION

You are the purchasing manager for Alpha Corporation. You are responsible for buying two $1 million generators. Your company has a written policy prohibiting any company buyer from receiving a gratuity in excess of $50 and requiring that all gratuities be reported. The company has no company policy regarding *whistle-blowing*. A salesperson for a generator manufacturer offers to arrange it so that you can buy a $12,000 car for $4,000. The car would be bought from a third party. You decline the offer.

Do you now report it to your superior? To the salesperson's superior?

The ethical problems presented in cases like these would be very difficult to resolve on the basis of traditional moral principles like "Do unto others as you would have them do unto you," which have a high degree of generality. However, by taking the perspective that sees fulfilling one's role as a starting point for acceptable legal and moral behavior, the issues at hand are much more manageable. The question we should ask is, "What are the moral duties that go with the job of auditor, consultant, and purchasing manager?" Once that question is settled, then a defensible, albeit still debatable, answer to the question of what one ought to do is in hand.

Consider the case of Alpha Corporation. If the purchasing manager had accepted the gratuity, the action would have violated both company policy and common morality, and hence it would have been wrong. In addition, if Alpha Corporation had had a policy requiring whistle-blowing, the manager would have acted wrongly to have violated company policy by remaining silent. But there is no such explicit policy. This is similar to the situation in colleges where there is an honor code. There is a greater responsibility to report cheating in a school with an honor code than there is in a school without an honor code. But in Alpha Corporation there is no such explicit policy. One may then ask whether there is an *unofficial policy* that requires whistle-blowing. Many of our associates in business who have considered this case have indicated that such an unofficial policy does indeed exist in their companies. To the extent that such an unofficial policy does exist, then there is some moral obligation not to remain silent. Should there be neither an official nor an unofficial policy in favor of whistle-blowing, then the moral obligation to whistle-blow must be an obligation that is outside one's role as purchasing manager.

Similar considerations arise in the case of the engineering consultant. His job was to evaluate the mine, which he did. His report included the disclosure of Surestrike's infringement on the property of West Virginia Mining. Is it part of the job of a consultant to get one's employers to act morally? Where could we find an answer to that question? An obvious place to start is with the code of ethics of the society that represents professional engineers. If such a rule appeared in the code, then the engineer has a significant reason for believing that he has an obligation to blow the whistle on Surestrike. If the rule does not appear, the issue is more cloudy.

Such discussions are not merely academic. Following the Equity Funding scandal among others, the accounting profession was under severe criticism for not exposing fraudulent client practices. Clearly accountants have obligations of confidentiality to their clients. But recently, public pressure has been extensive in trying to influence both an amendment to the code of ethics of accountants and in developing an unofficial expectation that accountants would make public fraudulent activities of the firms that they audit. In this case public expectations of the moral elements of the accountant's role are becoming more stringent. Much more will be said about what a code of ethics should contain and what function codes of ethics have in securing morally appropriate business practices.

Still, it is clear that a first responsibility is to do one's job, to fulfill the obligations associated with one's role. Once we move from those fairly clear role obligations we must make appeal to general moral expectations. There may be an expectation that people will report felonies, and Surestrike's infringement might be a felony. But that is an obligation of an engineer as a private citizen; it is not clear that it is an obligation of the engineer as an engineer.

JUSTIFYING THE ROLE-MORALITY APPROACH

We have been saying that in taking a job one assumes duties, responsibilities, and obligations that are attached to the vocational role that one assumes. But how can we show, more formally, that there is a moral duty to fulfill one's role? What general reasons or principle can be appealed to? To show how this might be done we need to turn our attention to two great theoretical ethical traditions to see how they justify the claim that one "should" (morally should) fulfill the duties attached to one's role. These two traditions are named, respectively, the *deontological* and the *utilitarian*.

Just briefly, an action can be evaluated either by looking at the consequences of the action or at the structure and motive of the action itself. Thus, one can decide that everyone should do one's job because one has promised to do it and one should keep promises, even if it is inconvenient, or one can decide that everyone ought to do one's job because the consequences of everyone becoming a gold-bricker would be disastrous for society. But one may ask on a more general level, "Why bother to keep promises?" We can either try to show that there is something in the very act of keeping promises that obliges us to keep our promises—a deontological approach—or we can try to show that the consequences of keeping promises are much better for society than are the consequences of everyone breaking promises—a utilitarian approach. These ethical, theoretical approaches offer an account of the most general prescriptions that govern our lives.

Deontological Ethics

The central thesis of deontological ethics is that consequences of actions are not the primary considerations in deciding what ought to be done. Rather, obligations, responsibilities, and considerations of justice and fairness take precedence. Our obligations and duties sometimes override desirable consequences. Desirable consequences do not justify an action or practice if it involves actions such as breaking promises, contracts, the agreements that one makes, or overturning the relations one has to those affected by one's actions. Businesses have a number of relationships, which were established through contracts, promises, and agreements, both explicit and understood, which carry their own responsibilities.

Suppose that the chief executive of a corporation is asked to make a sizable donation on the company's behalf to a university. The consequences of such a donation would probably be good for the community and for the university. But the deontological principle requires that the issue not be decided simply by determining whether the action has desirable consequences. After all, "The ends don't justify the means." Or thus a deontologist would argue. According to deontological theory, the chief executive must consider the impact of the gift on profits, because he or she has a fiduciary responsibility to the stockholders and also must consider both past agreements (Has the company promised support to this institution?) and the relation this company has to the university (Are many of its employees graduates? Does the company use the resources of the university?). In deciding what one should do, all these considerations need to be weighed.

According to deontological theory, the relationship one has to those affected by one's actions is a relevant consideration in determining what one ought to do. Thus, it follows that in assuming a job (a role), one also assumes special relations with one's employer and colleagues and as a result assumes moral obligations to the employer or colleagues. In other words, a deontologist would insist that one's role is a relevant factor in considering what one ought or ought not to do.

But a critic might persist. What reasons can a deontologist give in defense of selecting roles as one of the items to be considered in determining one's obligations? For one thing, one might satisfy the critic by pointing out that meeting one's role responsibilities is part of ordinary moral expectations, moral phenomena that we encounter by examining either our common moral practices or the moral language we all agree on. For example, we admire "a person of his (or her) word." We expect "promises to be kept, no matter what." That's what promises are all about. We often admire people of "principle" who see a course of action through no matter what the consequences. Now ethical theories should explain these common moral phenomena, and both our moral language and our moral practices support the contention that at least some moral obligations arise as a result of the roles or positions one has. Being a parent does impose obligations on the parent. Thus, deontological ethical theory incorporates society's view of the importance of role as an element in deciding the actual obligations one has.

Specifically in the case of business roles, we could show that people should perform their role because they have promised to do so. A promise is a freely entered into agreement, and deontologists insist, for a variety of reasons we need not spell out here, that promises should be kept.

Utilitarian Ethics

Another justification for role morality is provided by the other great tradition in ethical theory—the utilitarian tradition. Remembering that there are actions and consequences to consider in any ethical action, the utilitarian takes the consequences to be of paramount importance. Indeed, the utilitarian might be inclined to say, "If the end doesn't justify the means, what in the world does? If an action isn't going to lead to some good, why do it?" For a utilitarian, what one ought to do is determined solely by the consequences that result. One ought to act so as to bring about the best consequences one can for everyone affected by the action. So, if we are to justify role morality on utilitarian grounds, we need to show that if individuals holding roles assume obligations that go with those roles, good consequences will result; that is, the practice of responsibly fulfilling one's role will lead to a better society.

Let us again consider parenthood. It is a practical impossibility to be equally concerned with all the world's children. Children as a whole would be better off if parents were given primary responsibilities for the care of the children they had. Hence, the view that the parent role places on the parent special obligations to one's children is justified on utilitarian grounds. So it is with other roles or positions in life. If people mind their business and meet the responsibilities associated with their job, the whole society will be better off. This utilitarian consideration is exactly what is behind the idea of a "division of labor." If all people take responsibility for their own roles, then society will flourish. To the extent that role morality is like a division of labor, it is justified by utilitarians because role morality appears to lead to good consequences.

ROLE CONFLICT AND CONFLICTING ROLES

An obvious problem with role morality is the existence of conflicts. Problems arise on two fronts. A problem might arise because a role we occupy may have conflicting obligations, or because one of the roles we play may conflict with other roles that make a moral claim on us. It is obvious that our roles are not limited to the job we have. If one is a parent, one ought to fulfill the duties of parenthood, and in fulfilling those duties one is a good parent. If one is a bricklayer, one ought to fulfill those duties associated with the trade of bricklaying, and by fulfilling those duties one is a good bricklayer. Thus, part of being a good person is carrying out the obligations and responsibilities of one's various roles. But it is no doubt obvious that the duties of these various roles can conflict. For example, what if you have a job to do and a sick child to take care of? That is, what if your job responsibilities conflict with other non-job-related responsibilities? What is the moral thing to do? Further, what if my job gives me conflicting responsibilities? What if you are a carpenter who takes pride in your work, but your boss only lets you use cheaper and less satisfactory materials? What ought one to do when the duties of a role conflict or when the duties of various roles come into conflict?

Some conflicts, as we said, arise internally within the job itself. At the beginning of this chapter a distinction was made among the cultural, legal, and moral components of any job. In addition to the official "employer-stated" expectations concerning job performance, there are also the unofficial "culturally based" expectations of one's colleagues or co-workers. Frequently, the official "employer" expectations come into conflict with the unofficial "co-worker" expectations. Management encourages maximum productivity. From that perspective, the best employee is the most productive employee. Co-workers hardly ever have much praise for the extraordinarily productive worker. A person who far exceeds the average is a serious threat. Management will soon wonder why others cannot produce as much. The pressure of less productive co-workers on extremely productive ones is enormous. Most highly productive workers succumb and their productivity falls. How should such conflicts be resolved?

Consider an even stickier conflict. Take an engineer who feels bound by allegiance to his employer not to blow the whistle on a dangerous construction practice that, nevertheless, meets federal safety standards (for example, the Ford Pinto case). How can we resolve these conflicts? Or take the stockbroker who agreed to sell certain stocks for an underwriter even after finding out that the stocks were not a very good buy. Who is the stockbroker responsible to, the clients or the underwriter?

But even more than these conflicts, there are others that occur between one's responsibilities to one's job and one's other role-related responsibilities—for example, to one's family, church, and state. These conflicts are particularly acute for young executives and those whose job responsibilities are open-ended, such as doctors, lawyers, real-estate agents, and university professors. A university professor could literally spend all his or her waking hours working—research is an open-ended task. Like housework, it is never done. Many jobs are like that. The more time one spends on the job, the less time one has available for other pursuits—many of which can also make moral demands on one's time.

The discussion of these conflicts is not the idle fantasizing of a philosopher—the discussion mirrors actual historical circumstances. Until recently, many corporations moved young executives from one part of the country to the other with great frequency, often at great emotional cost to spouses and children. New, highly paid M.B.A's are expected to work 60 or 70 hours a week. Some cabinet officials in both Democratic and Republican administrations pride themselves on their 16-hour days, 7-day-a-week workloads and expect immediate subordinates to follow a similar routine. Some corporations have placed restraints on the kinds of activities employees may pursue in off-hours. These restraints apply both to political and social activities. Certain residential areas are preferred over others. Expectations exist concerning the amount and style of entertaining. Of course, some people give too little to their jobs and hence fail to fulfill reasonable responsibilities, but others seem to give far too much to their jobs and hence fail to meet the obligations of their other roles. How much is a person required to do? How are the conflicting obligations to be balanced?

If we look at the question from the point of view of the employer or the principal, one could imagine that the employer would be happy to receive unflagging loyalty to the firm on the part of the employee or agent. David Ewing sees this demand for loyalty written into the agency laws themselves. As he notes:

> To leave absolutely no doubt that employers and union managers can demand complete loyalty from subordinates and get it, the common law says the employer may discharge his employee at any time for any reason, so long as there is no statute or agreement limiting such right of discharge. A fortiori, the employer can transfer, promote, demote, or otherwise change an employee's status at any time. It does not matter if the boss is arbitrary or even wrong in taking such action. He doesn't have to give a good reason or any reason.[9]

In business it is imperative, if business is to function well, for superiors and managers to get people to do their bidding. A feeling of loyalty works very well in getting people to do more than they are contractually obliged to do. Thus, loyalty would seem to be a good thing to keep a company going, and many would claim that there is some minimal obligation of loyalty to the company, or that one of the chief duties of an employee (agent) is loyalty to the employer (principal). Many business people consider loyalty the chief duty of any employee, and many corporate executives or board members or CEOs feel they cannot overemphasize the importance of loyalty. Management consultants stress the necessity of instilling feelings of loyalty in employees. And as a matter of fact, one's work very often takes on meaning when one has great loyalty to the company.

But loyalty to one's job is certainly not sufficient. There are limits to loyalty. Suppose one is loyal to an immoral cause or end. After all, there is loyalty among thieves. One should perhaps be loyal to one's job, or firm, or boss (there are arguments that these sorts of things are not the proper kind of objects to be loyal to; loyalty should be to people), but it is certainly the case that the virtue of loyalty does not require that one accept blindly the person or cause to which one is loyal. To be loyal to an employer does not require blind loyalty; it does not require that the employee should do what the employer says come what may. Regrettably, however, it is just this kind of blind loyalty that some employers demand. Examples come immediately to mind of executives being asked to lie about product quality, delivery dates, or estimated costs of future prices. Employees sometimes are asked to carry out racist, sexist, ageist, or non-ecological policies or processes. In portions of the business world, an institutionalized program of rebates, "kickbacks," and "considerations" still remains, which many employees find morally repugnant, yet they are asked to carry out the *sub rosa* policies. Engineers sometimes comment about the professional and personal anger and anxiety they feel at being asked to design products that they know to be deficient in a number of ways.

A Higher Morality

Suppose an employer in the name of loyalty makes unethical or illegal requests? Consider the example at the beginning of this chapter. Is Mr. Norwood entitled to one's loyalty? In general, should an employee be loyal and carry out unethical or illegal requests? Not if there are universal moral norms that supersede the duties associated with one's role. This leads us to the last question of this chapter: Is there a higher morality that supersedes role morality in any of its forms?

If there are external roles that conflict, which role is to be followed? It would seem that a higher morality needs to be appealed to in order to determine which role obligations take priority. There are those who say that business ethics deals with simply what one must do if one is to be a good business person. Others argue that to be a good person is to go beyond being a good business person. Perhaps the entire discussion can be summarized in the following way: Business ethics begins with the duties associated with one's role in business, but business ethics certainly does not end there. A full theory of business ethics must determine which specific duties associated with one's business roles are morally or ethically legitimate, how the conflict of duties within one's roles are to be resolved, when the duties associated with one's business role ought to be superseded by duties associated with other roles one might hold, and finally when the demands of morality, not associated in any way with roles, supersede the morality of roles. In the next chapter we deal with the first of these important issues: What are the duties associated with one's role in business?

To answer that question we need to look at business itself. If one of my roles is to be a good business person, it is important to know what the purpose or function of business is, so that as a loyal employee I can help my firm fulfill its purpose. We turn, then, to the question, What is the function or purpose of a corporation?

NOTES

[1]Dorothy Emmet, *Rules, Roles, and Relations* (Boston: Beacon Press, 1966), 15.

[2]R.S. Downie, *Roles and Values: An Introduction to Social Ethics* (London: Methuen & Co., 1971), 128.

[3]"The term *agency* is used to describe the fiduciary relationship that exists when one person acts on behalf and under the control of another person." Robert N. Corley, Peter J. Shedd, and Eric M. Holmes, *Principles of Business Law* Thirteenth Edition (Englewood Cliffs, NJ: Prentice Hall, 1986), p. 295.

[4]F.H. Bradley, *Ethical Studies* (Indianapolis: Bobbs-Merrill Co., 1951), 136.

[5]Charles Fried, *Right and Wrong* (Cambridge, Mass.: Harvard University Press, 1978), 168.

[6]Hannah Arendt, *The Human Condition* (Chicago: University of Chicago Press, 1958), Chapters 3 & 4.

[7]Emmet, *Rules, Roles, and Relations*, 159.

[8]These two cases are taken from material developed by the Committee for Education in Business Ethics under a grant from the National Endowment for the Humanities.

[9]David W. Ewing, *Freedom Inside the Organization: Bringing Civil Liberties to the Workplace* (New York: E.P. Dutton, 1977), 30. Recent court cases have slightly modified this once absolute right of employers to fire employees.

Chapter Two

The Moral Responsibilities
of Business

In the last chapter we saw that morality has to do with answering the question "What should one do?" and that one of the things we should do is to fulfill the responsibilities of our role. Thus, a business person has obligations to fulfill in order to be judged a good business person. But this same person has other roles to fulfill, such as friendship roles and family roles, which can conflict with one's business roles. What should one do in such cases of conflict? For example, what if a business person has to decide whether or not to fire an old friend who is not producing enough and costing the company money? How does one choose between loyalty to an old friend and the responsibility to turn a profit? What should be done in such a case? How can such conflicts be resolved?

THREE POSITIONS ON BUSINESS AND ETHICS

The way one resolves such conflicts will depend very much on how one views the relationship between business and ethics. There are basically three views. The first is that ethics has nothing to do with business; the second is that business has a special role to fulfill in society, and if business priorities are allowed to rule over other conflicting obligations, the business person will benefit society; the final view is that business interests must at times bow to other moral concerns; that is, morality at times rules over business.

The first view, the view that denies ethics has anything to do with business, doesn't resolve the issue so much as simply give priority to the business decision: "Business is business and shouldn't be mixed up with ethics." Holders of this view would say things like, "When in Rome do as the Romans do." Thus, when you are at work, do business, and when you are at home worry about loyalty to friends or other ethical matters. On this view ethics and morality are largely private matters that have no relation to business. Business is a tough game, and you don't have to get into it, but if you do, you'd better have the stomach to live with the decisions you will have to make. Proponents of this view sometimes maintain that "business ethics" is an oxymoron, a contradiction in terms, like "jumbo shrimp." "If you want to be ethical, join a monastery or be a teacher, but if you want to get into business, recognize it's a tough, dog-eat-dog, competitive world where there's no room for softies or bleeding hearts."

The second view is a bit more subtle than the first. It maintains that the sole purpose of business is to make a profit, but it justifies business's single-minded pursuit of profit on moral grounds. It makes a utilitarian claim that if business doesn't deviate from pursuing a profit, then society will be better off. Thus, business people, in fulfilling their role obligations for their own sake and the sake of their business, serendipitously make society better off too. The business person's role in society is crucial, and even though other roles conflict with it, in the long run just performing the correct business practices will be the ethical thing for the business person to do. Since good business is good ethics, good ethics will be good business too. So, even if you need to be tough, you can take heart in knowing that society will be better off because someone is doing the dirty jobs. If we don't lay off the old friends, the company will go under, and then more people will be out of work.

The final view maintains that pursuing the most efficient, most profitable business practice is not always the correct way to proceed. At times pursuing the ethical course of action will require pursuing a less profitable course of action. Ethically, there are times a person is obliged to set aside profit considerations in order to prevent harm or to accomplish some social good. There is more to business than merely making a profit. Businesses produce "goods" or provide services to people. They create jobs and hence business accepts some responsibility to make society better. This last view seems to be the most commonly accepted one of the relation of ethics to business today. But showing that it is correct and detailing under what conditions business people should override their obligations to profit making for the sake of some other social good will be a large part of this book.

Actions, Practices, and Institutions: An Important Distinction

In order to examine and evaluate these three positions critically it is important to make a distinction among three different objects that ethics evaluates: (1) individual actions, "Should John lie to make this sale?" (2) social practices, "Is the common practice of lying [if it is a practice] to make a sale an acceptable business practice?" and (3) social institutions, "Is the business system of corporations and firms, which is set up to make a profit, a defensible way of organizing society?" It is important to realize that the business system is a social institution, with a history that was devised by human beings for specific purposes. The business system, as we know it, did not exist when human beings first walked the earth. It was a long time coming and has just recently, in the past two hundred years, developed as we now know it. If the system that developed is a bad social institution it can be reformed or replaced.

Thus, we have three questions. Is the system itself, ordinarily called the *capitalist system,* a morally defensible system? If it is, then a second question arises: Are certain practices, such as buying and selling, keeping accounts, making agreements, advertising, employing, firing etc., morally defensible? Finally, there are individual, particular business actions, such as buying this particular product at this time, making this particular deal at this time, etc. What standards govern these actions? Are they proper? According to what rules?

Initially, we will examine the institution of business itself to see whether or not morality should be applied to business at all and, if it should, in what way? To do that, we will have to examine the purpose of business and its vehicle—the for-profit corporation. If its sole purpose is profit maximization, we will need to examine whether an institution with profit maximization as its primary goal is a desirable kind of institution. Thereafter, we will examine the moral requirements that govern various business practices, and what duties and responsibilities businesses have to their various constituencies. Finally, we will examine the question of what would motivate business to fulfill its moral obligations. Is government regulation the only way to get business to meet its moral responsibilities? Why be moral if the government doesn't demand it or prudence doesn't dictate it?

But before we do any of that, it is probably prudent to answer some skeptical doubts about the legitimacy of business ethics in the first place. After all, what's the point of applying ethics to those three tiers of questions if it's all a lot of hogwash. So, to begin let's see if we can dispose of the old cliche that "There is no such thing as business ethics."

THERE ARE NO RESPONSIBILITIES

Perhaps the strongest arguments for this position are those of Albert Carr in a now almost classical article, "Is Business Bluffing Ethical?" According to Carr, there may be something called ethics, but that is a matter for one's personal life, and it ought not to be confused with the ethics or rules one follows in doing business. Business may have a set of rules that participants play by, and that might be a kind of "ethics" of business, but it has nothing to do with the ethics governing the morals of everyday life. Carr views business as a competitive enterprise, much like a poker game. The purpose of the game is to win, and as long as one plays by the acceptable rules of the game, rules quite different from ethical rules emphasizing cooperation and concern for others, then one's behavior is all right. One might say that whereas the first rule of morality is "Do unto others as you would have them do unto you," in the competitive game of business, just like in the game of poker, the primary rule is "Do unto others what you *wouldn't* have them do to you, before they do it to you." As Carr observes:

Poker's own brand of ethics is different from the ethical ideals of civilized human relationships. The game calls for distrust of the other fellow. It ignores the claim of friendship. Cunning deception and concealment of one's strength and intentions, not kindness and openheartedness, are vital in poker. No one thinks any worse of poker on that account. And no one should think any worse of the game of business because its standards of right and wrong differ from the prevailing traditions of morality in our society.[1]

Carr continues:

That most businessmen are not indifferent to ethics in their private lives, everyone will agree. My point is that in their office lives they cease to be private citizens; they become game players who must be guided by a somewhat different set of standards.... [T]he golden rule, for all its value as an ideal for society, is simply not feasible as a guide for business. A good part of the time the businessman is trying to do unto others as he hopes others will not do unto him. [2]

Carr sums up in the following way what he believes to be the prevailing attitude of businesspersons toward ethics:

We live in what is probably the most competitive of the world's civilized societies. Our customs encourage a high degree of aggression in the individual's striving for success. Business is our main area of competition, and it has been ritualized into a game of strategy. The basic rules of the game have been set by the government, which attempts to detect and punish business frauds. But as long as a company does not transgress the rules of the game set by law, it has the legal right to shape its strategy without reference to anything but its profits. If it takes a long-term view of its profits, it will preserve amicable relations, so far as possible with those with whom it deals. A wise businessman will not seek advantage to the point where he generates dangerous hostility among employees, competitors, customers, government, or the public at large. But decisions in this area are, in the final test, decisions of strategy, not of ethics....[Thus] If a man plans to take a seat in the *business game* he owes it to himself to master the principles by which the game is played, including its special ethical outlook.[3]

There is much that strikes us as correct about what Carr is saying. Business life is, in many respects, like playing poker. In business life there are acceptable rules for winning and losing, and there are certain practices that must be obeyed, and there are even skillful moves and nonskillful moves. There is competition, and bluffing, and outsmarting, etc.

The chief difficulty with Carr's position is that he construes morality or ethics in a very narrow way. An ethic for him is simply a set of rules or practices that one obeys. But different sets of rules exist for different circumstances. There is an ethics governing one's private life and the responsibilities one has toward one's family, friends, and social acquaintances, as well as a different ethic for one's business life, governing how one is going to make money. For Carr, as we said, if the two sets of practices conflict, simply follow the business practices. Thus, Carr answers the problem of conflict by simply requiring business people to do what is good for business.

But why should one's role as a business person take precedence over all one's other roles? To leave it there puts the business person in a terrible bind. If one's personal "morality" is such that it conflicts with business practices, that person either has to suppress that morality or give up business. But why should that have to be the case? Carr doesn't have an answer, except perhaps to shrug and say, "That's just the way it is." Such a response won't do.

When we look closely at Carr we see that what he does is adopt a not so subtle form of the anti-ethical theory called *ethical relativism*. Ethical relativism is a theory which maintains two things: 1) that every social group has its own set of moral beliefs and 2) that those beliefs are correct for that group. The theory arises from observations of anthropologists who make it clear that different cultures have different sets of moral beliefs. If that was all there was to ethical relativism there would be no problem, for relativism would simply be asserting the well known fact that different cultures have different rules. But the second clause, "that those rules are correct for that group" goes much further. If that is the case, individual societies make their own rules and there are no trans-cultural principles that allow one to judge one society's set of rules as better than another's. Popularly this is expressed by saying "When in Rome do as the Romans do." Although we are inclined to judge others by our standards, relativists argue that to do so is ethno-centric. Relativism promotes pluralism and tolerance, which are undoubtedly good things, but it has its drawbacks.

First, some societies have bad practices, and the fact that they think those practices are correct doesn't make us concur. In the United States we hold that bribery is an unacceptable business practice, even in countries whose rules or customs permit it. But if we are correct in our belief, the other culture's thinking that they are right about bribery doesn't make them right any more than Nazis' thinking the holocaust was justified were right. Thinking something is right and its being right are different things.

Other difficulties with ethical relativism are determining what constitutes a social group, as well as who speaks for the group. Obviously if each society determines what's right or wrong for its members we have to know who is included. Is a society a nation, an ethnic group, a family or possibly even a community within a nation like the business community? But even if we determine what a group is, who decides what rules a group holds? The majority? The minority? Or some authoritarian leader? How large must a group be? Is a family too small? Is a group of one a possibility? Finally, which group's rules does one obey if a person belongs to more than one group?

Here we see how Carr's theory is relativistic. Carr notes that we belong to several groups. Our family and religious groups give us sets of moral rules, but they do not apply when we join our other group, the business world. That world has different rules and they are correct for that group. Hence Carr is an implicit relativist. Hence he faces the problems any relativist does. Who speaks for the business community? What does one do when the business rules conflict with other groups' rules? Why would business' rules get priority? What if business people disagree about the right thing to do? And finally, when do my rules from my other groups cease to bind me? When I leave my house in the morning? When I get on the train? Or is it only when I walk into the office building?

Saying that business has its own set of rules is unacceptable, because it doesn't resolve the question of whether business' practices are morally acceptable or not.

Besides, Carr's relativism, we can also question the adequacy of his analogy of business with poker. Carr's analogy of business with poker is fine as far as it goes, but it doesn't go far enough. Consider: Poker is a game with its own set of rules where one drops out of everyday matters for a while. In a game one's friend becomes one's "opponent"; and the object of the game is to defeat the opponent. That is certainly not the object of all relations in life nor does it seem to be the object of all business relations.

Second, one shouldn't play poker if one doesn't have the money to cover losses, or if one has to be elsewhere. That is, there are moral rules that govern whether one should play poker at all. If there are rules governing when and who should be able to play poker and under what circumstances, then there is the possibility of rules governing when and who should be permitted to "play the game" of business.

There is another problem with the poker analogy. All the players in a poker game are free participants in the game. In the business world, however, all people, or the vast majority, can't help but be involved with business and business practices. Nearly all people are part of the economy. They cannot leave the table whenever they wish. If the business players are only the business "magnates" of the world, then there would be no moral problem in their trying to beat each other. But that's not the case. Others are affected by their game. For example, if two high stakes gamblers are involved in a corporate takeover struggle and the "winner" needs to gut the company by firing workers after the takeover, those workers who were innocent bystanders are affected by the game. They are "losers" without even a chance of sitting down at the table. Thus, a better analogy would be one that noted that the fortunes of the players affect others not at the game. If losing at the poker table costs my family, the rules of poker are overriden by concerns other than those internal to the game.

Carr implicitly recognizes this, for he insists that the game be governed by law and the government. But the government's laws are legitimated and evaluated in terms of their fairness and justice, in terms of how they provide for the common good and individual welfare. But such laws are based on moral considerations that override the internal rules of the business game. To the extent that law and morals constrain business, business resembles less and less the game of poker.

THE RESPONSIBILITY OF BUSINESS IS TO MAKE A PROFIT

Perhaps we can see more clearly how business comes under ethics by using the following example. Suppose there was a group of outlaws who murdered and pillaged. They would have to live according to rules, have a leader, and keep promises to one another and trust each other or they wouldn't be a very good group of outlaws. But the fact that they are good outlaws doesn't justify their outlawry. No, the practice of outlawry must be justified on its own. Most outlaws do bad things. Only exceptionally do we find an outlaw like Robin Hood, whose behavior we justify by the good he does for the downtrodden. In short, if an institution or practice is no good, then one should not join it. There are those who will say that the very institution of business is bad. If so, then business itself is unethical in its very being. Let's examine this claim and see whether the moral probity of the business enterprise can be defended.

In order to do that, we should first examine what business is. It is important to note that business is an institution, a system set up by human beings to get things done. It has a purpose. Thus, business, as a social institution or a convention, is not a natural thing.

In ordinary conversation, we often make reference to a good knife, a good racehorse, or a good investment. In going to the grocery store, we want to pick out a good head of lettuce and get a good buy at the meat counter. Suppose that we were asked to explain our use of "good" in each of these contexts. We would answer the question by appealing to the function or purpose of the thing or activity in question. For example, a good knife is sharp so that it can fulfill its function of cutting well. A good head of lettuce has those qualities that make it good to eat. There seems to be a connection between being a good X and X's fulfilling its function.

Early Greek philosophy built an entire ethical theory on this insight. Both Plato and Aristotle agreed that a good X is an X that fulfills its function or purpose. Just as knives, racehorses, and investments had purposes, so did human beings, institutions, and even states. The purpose of human beings was to develop and to integrate all human capacities. In Plato and Aristotle's view, a person's rational capacities held the most important place in the process of integration and development.

Suppose we apply this way of thinking to corporations. We would first ask what the purpose of a corporation is and then ask whether this purpose is a good one. If we find that it has a good or defensible purpose, then we can go on to examine the right and wrong, good and bad ways of carrying out this legitimate purpose.

Perhaps the most famous statement of the classical theory of business and the consequent defense of that theory is that of Milton Friedman.

Friedman asserts that in a free society "there is one and *only one* social responsibility of business—to use its resources and engage in activities designed to increase its profits as long as it stays within the rules of the game, which is to say, engages in open and free competition without deception and fraud."[4] The purpose of a business is to engage in activities designed to increase its profits.

If this purpose of business is worthwhile, anyone working for it has an obligation to aid in fulfilling its purpose. Friedman further maintains that

> In a free enterprise, private-property system a corporate executive is an employee of the owners of the business. He has direct responsibility to his employers. That responsibility is to conduct the business in accordance with their desires, which generally will be to make as much money as possible while conforming to the basic rules of the society, both those embodied in law and

> those embodied in ethical custom. Of course, in some cases his employers may have a different objective. A group of persons might establish a corporation for an eleemosynary purpose—for example, a hospital or a school. The manager of such a corporation will not have money profit as his objective but the rendering of certain services.
>
> In either case, the key point is that, in his capacity as a corporate executive, the manager is the agent of the individuals who own the corporation or establish the eleemosynary institution, and his primary responsibility is to them.[5]

Thus, according to Friedman, the *sole* purpose of a business is to make a profit, and the obligation of the manager as an agent of the company is to make money for the company if it is a for-profit business.

This account of the purpose of business is certainly familiar and is imbedded in the basic beliefs of our society. Consider the following example. Suppose I had a million dollars to start a business. After getting the business on its feet, I hired you to run it and retired to Florida to golf and enjoy myself. When I returned and asked you for an accounting, you told me there were no profits because the people of the community needed recreational facilities and you took whatever surplus cash there was and donated it to their cause. Is that what you were hired for? Of course not. You were hired to make money for me.

This purpose of business has also been established as a precedent in law. At first the courts interpreted "maximize profits" in a very narrow sense. In the famous case of *Dodge* v. *Ford Motor Co.* (1919), the court required Henry Ford to increase the dividends he paid to his stockholders. The court overturned management decisions made by Ford on the grounds that stockholder rights had been violated.

The record, and especially the testimony of Mr. Ford,

> convinces that he has to some extent the attitude towards shareholders of one who has disposed and distributed to them large gains and that they should be content to take what he chooses to give. His testimony creates the impression, also that he thinks the Ford Motor Company has made too much money, has had too large profits, and that although large profits might still be earned, a sharing of them with the public by reducing the price of the output of the company, ought to be undertaken....There should be no confusion (of which there is evidence) of the duties which Mr. Ford conceives that he and the stockholders owe to protesting, minority stockholders. A business corporation is organized and carried on primarily for the profit of the stockholders. The powers of the directors are to be employed for that end. The discretion of directors is to be exercised in the choice of means to attain that end and does not extend to a change in the end itself, to the reduction of profits or to the nondistribution of profits among stockholders in order to devote them to other purposes.[6]

Later, the courts seemed to overrule the precedent of *Dodge* v. *Ford Motor Co.* In the classic case of *A.P. Smith Manufacturing Co.* v. *Barlow* (1953), the court permitted charitable donations to Princeton University. Although the decision in this case is widely regarded as revolutionizing the flexibility of corporate managers and boards to seek ends beyond profits, a careful reading of the judge's opinion suggests an evolution rather than a revolution. The presiding judge still accepted the view that the function of a corporation was to maximize profits, but it was long-run profits rather than immediate profits that should count. Judge Stein's opinion is worth quoting at length.

> I cannot conceive of any greater benefit to corporations in this country than to build, and continue to build, respect for and adherence to a system of free enterprise and democratic government, the serious impairment of either of which may well spell the destruction of all corporate enterprise. Nothing that aids or promotes the growth and service of the American university or college in respect of the matter here discussed can possibly be anything short of direct benefit to every corporation in the land. The college-trained men and women are a ready reservoir from which industry may draw to satisfy its need for scientific or executive talent. It is no answer to say that a company is not as benefited unless such need is immediate. A long-range view must be taken of the matter. A small company today might be under no imperative requirement to engage the services of a research chemist or other scientist, but its growth in a few years may be such that it must have available an ample pool from which it may obtain the needed service.[7]

Ever since this decision, corporations have moved with increasing boldness into activities that clearly reduce profits in the short run. However, the law requires that corporations be prepared to show that any activity enhances long-term profits.

But the fact that there are laws specifying the purpose of a corporation doesn't show that those laws establish a good institution nor do they show how such an institution developed. This history of the development of business as a system for profits is a fascinating one, but it is too long to be told here. Suffice it to say that for such a system to develop, society had to value "profit."

During the seventeenth and eighteenth centuries, philosophers such as Thomas Hobbes, John Locke, and Adam Smith studied human nature and claimed that the best economic system for society would be one that recognized individual self-interest. But isn't concern for one's self-interest the very heart of behavior that conflicts with ethical behavior? This appeal to self-interest called for a defense. What was devised was a defense of the classical theory of economics on utilitarian grounds. In short, Adam Smith in *The Wealth of Nations* (1776) claimed that if we all pursued our own business interests, society would be better served. An "invisible hand" coordinated individual self-interested behavior so that social good resulted.

You are probably familiar with contemporary arguments along these lines. Capitalism, the system of business, freely engaged in making profits, has produced the highest standard of living in history.

The Utilitarian Defense

As you will recall, utilitarianism maintains that an action, practice, or system is good and justifiable in proportion as it tends to lead to good consequences. In order to defend the institution of business on utilitarian grounds, we need to show that the institution of business leads to the greatest good for the greatest number of people.

Corporations are creations of the state, and since the state is responsible for the general welfare, we assume it allowed the maximizing of profit to be the goal or the purpose of the corporation on the assumption that such a system would benefit society. Now any prediction of what will make people happy must rest on some psychological beliefs and empirical hypotheses about human nature and what motivates human beings. The state, then, at least implicitly assumed certain empirical hypotheses about human nature. We suggest that the state adopted two hypotheses in its belief that society in general would benefit if it allowed an institution such as a profit corporation to function.

One of these hypotheses is the psychological assumption that men and women are motivated primarily, if not solely, by self-interest. People's main concern is looking out for number one—or number one plus immediate relatives. The theory of motivation described here is given the name *psychological egoism*. In discussing psychological egoism, it should be emphasized that psychological egoism is not to be identified either with the view that humans are motivated to seek instant gratification or with the view that all humans are motivated by selfish impulses. Enlightened egoists know that tonight's drinking party is followed by tomorrow's headache and that overtly selfish behavior is usually self-defeating and hence imprudent. In other words, enlightened egoists will behave most times as do all socially responsible and well-behaved people.

The second empirical hypothesis associated with the utilitarian defense is exhibited in the classical economist Adam Smith's doctrine of the "invisible hand." Smith (1723–1790) recognized that not all interests of all individuals could be achieved. People cannot have everything they want. Inevitably there is competition among people as they try to achieve their interests. As long as there is a government to enforce the rules of the competitive game, the competitive process is orderly and efficient. Because people look after their own interests more effectively than they look after the interests of others, the rule-governed competitive struggle will lead to the greatest good for the greatest number. In this way one can say that enlightened self-interest (egoism) constrained by limited government leads to utilitarian results.

By making these two empirical assumptions explicit, one can now see why competition has been valued positively in business culture. Business recognizes that the material goods and services that people desire neither exist ready-made in nature nor are available in great abundance. Material goods must be produced from scarce commodities. Since the means for satisfying our desires are scarce, efficiency in production is highly valued. A competitive situation in which individuals struggle against one another to satisfy their own interests will be most efficient. In a competitive system where goods and services are not provided but rather are earned, people will have an incentive not only to work but to work hard. Competition molds character and contributes to utilitarian results. Welfare, on the other hand, is assumed to promote sloth, which is dangerous to the public good.

In summarizing this point, the classical view that a corporation's purpose is to maximize profits is justified on a utilitarian base. Utilitarian moral philosophers argue that institutions should be designed to maximize good consequences.

If it is true that human motivation has the character of enlightened self-interest, and if the invisible hand operating through a rule-governed competitive process really works, then as corporations seek to maximize profits, the greatest public good will result.

Critique of the Utilitarian Justification of Classical Theory

But there are those who argue that a system which allows business to have for its sole purpose the making of a profit will not always lead to the greatest good. Therefore the business system as we know it cannot be proven to be acceptable on utilitarian grounds. Critics of the classical theory would say that the utilitarian defense is based on the flawed empirical assumption about self-interested pursuits being guided by an invisible hand to produce public good.

Let us examine this counterargument. Although few doubt the prominence of self-interest in human motivation, the notion of the invisible hand is particularly vulnerable to attack. What the defenders of the invisible hand fail to notice is that the competitive process with its unchecked self-interest is, by itself, not sufficient to yield the greatest good for the greatest number. Cooperation is a necessary complement for achieving the public good. Indeed, Adam Smith's recognition that the competitive process must be governed by rules enforced by political authority provides the starting point for such an analysis. Smith recognized that a decent social life requires that we agree to constrain our self-seeking activities in accordance with the rules. A less optimistic precursor of Smith, the English philosopher Thomas Hobbes (1588–1679), argued that in an egoistic world, some rules are required if chaos is to be avoided. In a completely egoistic world without any rules, a state of nature would exist that would be characterized by a war of all against all. In such a world an individual's life would be "nasty, brutish and short." Thus, Smith would need a very powerful political authority to limit egoistic behavior—greed as Hobbes called it.

Even more important than the need to regulate competition for the greater public good, cooperation is needed in order to maximize happiness. We can illustrate the necessity of cooperative behavior by applying game theory to a competitive sales office situation. Suppose that in a sales division of 20 employees, word is received that, if overall performance of the sales unit continues to be high, an additional attractive management position will be added to the unit. Suppose that all 20 salespersons desire the new position and hence enter into competition for it. Let us suppose further that the current high performance of the sales department depends on the ability to discover new customers for one another. For example, one sales representative will always tell another about a prospective client in the other's neighborhood. Now that competition has begun for the new position, the sales representatives try to lure customers away from one another. Each salesperson would now try to gain any client for his or her account, even if that prospective client were a neighbor or friend of another in the unit. Since this salesperson is neither a neighbor nor a friend, he or she is less likely to obtain the account. Such a strategy when viewed as a unit is self-defeating; the requisite condition that overall performance of the sales unit remain high will not be met.

On the other hand, with such a competitive situation for the management position in effect, it would not be in the interest of any one salesperson to avoid trying to lure a customer account away from the other. He or she would certainly lose out on the competition for the new management position. What is needed, of course, is a binding rule of cooperation that says that each salesperson must give prospective clients to neighbors or friends of other sales representatives in the unit. Only if this rule is adopted will the end result that everyone wants—namely, the new management position—be attainable. Utilitarian results are not brought about simply by the existence of the invisible hand. The rules that govern the competitive process are equally important. If the rules are insufficient in number, inadequate in content, or not enforced, the public good will not be achieved. The traditional business view has overemphasized the benefits of competition and has underemphasized the benefits of cooperative rules.

A second argument against the utilitarian defense is that there are many goods and services that cannot be produced in sufficiently desired amounts through the competitive market process. Thus, for the market to work efficiently, one must presume that people express their true preferences in bidding for scarce goods and resources. This assumption works well enough for any commodity where my consumption precludes your consumption. Since you cannot eat the orange I have eaten, you will express your true preference for the orange and outbid me if you can. But consider a well-paved highway where my travel does not preclude yours. When it is time for highway repairs, it is in my self-interest to understate the worth of the highway to me. After all, I will still retain all my benefits if I can get other highway users to pay more. Of course, each highway user reasons as I do, and as a result the amount of money forthcoming for highway repairs is not equal to the collective desire of the community for well-paved highways. In this case, as in the case of other goods and services that resemble highways, the invisible hand of market competition cannot produce the public good.

Third, there are many by-products of business called *external diseconomies* that represent a cost borne by society although the cost was produced by business activity itself. Air and water pollution, excessive noise, and unattractive factories are some common examples. Unless these costs of doing business are taken into account, one gets a distortedly optimistic picture of the benefits of the competitive business enterprise. Even if a steel company would agree to pay the cost of its pollution, it is hard to see how on market grounds the costs could be assessed. Pollution is a product more like highways than like oranges. If the steel company asked those harmed by pollution how much they were harmed, they would try to overstate their harm, and hence the company would be penalized. Methods for determining and assessing the true costs of external diseconomies currently occupy the attention of many professional economists. As of this writing, however, there is no universally accepted solution to the problem.

Fourth, a large part of American corporate activity is not competitive—at least not competitive in the sense that Adam Smith and classical economists had in mind. For some products, like utility services, it is technically not feasible for competition to exist. In other industries (automobile production, for example), start-up costs for any potential firm are so prohibitive that competition is effectively stifled. Naturally, there is competition in the automobile industry, but not competition of the type you find among mom-and-pop grocery stores, or small factory owners specializing in, say, tool and die work. Moreover, as industries have grown, society is no longer able to allow the competitive process to work. Some companies, like some cities, cannot be allowed to go bankrupt, and hence society bails them out.

These four considerations lead us to doubt that the invisible hand that governs the competitive process is sufficient to produce utilitarian results. But even if these arguments don't give us pause, there is a problem endemic to utilitarianism that arises when it is used as a justification for classical economic theory—the problem of how the goods are to be distributed.

Basically, the classical view's utilitarian argument concentrates too much on the best way of increasing production, creating the maximum amount of goods, and ignores the problem of how those goods are to be distributed. For example, is it fair or just that in a society which produces the greatest gross national product in the history of the world, some people earn millions a year while others who work very hard subsist on only $3.35 an hour? An action or system cannot be justified simply on the grounds that it produces more than any other system. There must also be a concern that the goods produced get distributed fairly.

When faced with these criticisms, the defenders of the classical theory often turn in defense to a deontological ethical theory resting on the rights to liberty and property. These classical theorists view the rights to liberty and property as natural and inalienable. The free market system is viewed as the economic system that best defends those rights because in such a system people can make what they want and can buy what they want. Let us present the argument.

Defense of the Classical Theory from Property Rights

John Locke in the seventeenth century argued for the natural rights to life, liberty, and property, and he claimed that government's function was to defend these rights. Originally, Locke argued, everything except one's body was held in common, but one could gain possession of something by working for it. This possession made it one's property and gave one control over it. One also had the right to accumulate the property that one worked for in the form of money. This accumulation of money made capital possible, for capital is money that is used for investment purposes. Thus, one can take one's "capital" and start a business or factory, and since investors put their money to work they are entitled to the "profits" (the money over and above the fixed costs and wages paid that remains after the product is sold). Those people who band together to invest their money to start a business or support a business are the stockholders and owners. Managers and workers freely agree to work, not for the profit but for a wage determined by the "free market." The shareholders are then entitled to the profits, for they supposedly "risk" their investment in the "competitive" marketplace and "deserve" a reward. This arrangement has been legitimized by legal interpretation and has become politically accepted in terms of what some refer to as a "social contract." We can summarize the argument as follows: The shareholders own the corporation and consequently should decide to what end the company's profits should be used. People have a right to decide how they shall invest their own resources. When you add this property right claim to the empirical thesis that shareholders want corporations to maximize profits, the complete justification becomes clear. People have a right to decide how to use their property. The profit corporation is the property of the stockholders, and the stockholders want the corporation to maximize its profits. Since the stockholders have a right to use their property (the corporation) this way, the managers ought to seek to maximize profits. In short, the fact that business functions to make a profit is morally acceptable because it respects rights to freedom and property.

Critique of the Argument from Property Rights

The property argument that supports the moral acceptability of capitalism rests on several assumptions about property. A central tenet of capitalism is the right of owners of property to retain ownership of the output that emerges from the act of production.[8] An example will show clearly how this right works. If an owner of a factory makes a product, say a shoe, for a cost of $25, and sells it for $40, after deducting $5 for sales and marketing costs, the $10 left over is profit. Who is entitled to the profit? The standard answer, at least in capitalist countries, is the owners of the business, the factory in this case. They have "invested" their money, which "worked" for them in making the profit. The risks of their property and their entrepreneurial skill entitle them to ownership of the profit.

Marxists and other socialists would argue against this defense of capitalism because an insistence on such property rights allows the exploitation or use of human beings as commodities. Wages are really prices paid for the labor of human beings.

Further, Marxists and other socialists would ask where such a right comes from. According to them, the right to profits is not a natural right, for "profits," the surplus value created by the work of the laborer along with the entrepreneur, is a social invention and there cannot be natural rights attached to a human convention. Shouldn't the profit, which is the result of a joint venture—since nothing gets produced without workers—be shared? Marxists and other socialists see existing capitalist property arrangements as reflected in property laws as merely historical agreements worked out among powerful "owners" to keep control over the goods of the world that allow them to "exploit" the workers, the have-nots. On this view, rights are historical claims made by powerful classes against weak classes; in capitalism only might *makes* right. If the Marxists were entirely correct there would be no justification of business as it exists in a capitalist system.

Nevertheless, though capitalism is vulnerable with respect to the fairness of its distribution system, Marxist theory is notoriously shortsighted when it comes to understanding productive systems. Capitalists argue that unless they are rewarded for risking their money, there will be much less to be distributed and everyone will be worse off. Hence, capitalists argue that capitalism leaves more people better off than does any socialist economic system.

Still, the distribution problem is a serious one; a person does not need to be a Marxist or socialist to recognize it. According to Robert Heilbroner, an American economist, the defender of capitalism overlooks the imbalance of power that exists in most business relations.

> The reason is simple—in depicting "the economy" as the interaction of rational (self-interested) maximizers there is no place for conceiving it as a process that creates and distributes privilege and the capacity for domination as well as commodities. This is because the crucial social relationship of exchange takes place in a political vacuum. In this vacuum some offer "work" and others offer "employment." Both sides come together for the same rational, maximizing reasons, and the equality of their respective situations seems guaranteed by the fact that each side is free to reject the offer of the other. This view, however, overlooks a central asymmetry in the relationship of labor and capital. It is that sole title to the output—including the all-important element of profit that is normally realized from its sale—is lodged with the capitalist, not with the worker, even though the output is the product of the work of the one and the equipment of the other. Thus behind the seemingly equal legal footing of labor and capital underlies an overlooked inequality in their contractual prerogative.[9]

Capitalism, then, gives rise to large inequalities in power.

What all critics of the capitalist system agree on is that property rights are not unlimited. To understand this, consider the following distinctions that must be made concerning property rights.

Three possible positions can be taken with respect to the view of the relation of business to property.

1. Business should be privately owned and operated.
2. Business decisions should usually be private rather than public.
3. Business persons may do what they want with their property.

Most would take rules 1 and 2 as morally acceptable because of the good consequences business can produce. Rule 3 is the one that is under moral challenge.

Some critics or reformers of the classical capitalist system would hold there is no absolute right to do with one's property what one pleases. If I am selling my property, I cannot refuse to sell it to a black person. If I live in a development, I cannot own pigs or horses. If I own a swimming pool, it must be surrounded by a six-foot fence. If I own a pet rattlesnake, I cannot simply let it loose when I grow tired of it. Property rights are always limited rights.

Critics would also make a distinction between property for use and investment property. Investment property is different from other private property. Most stockholders in a corporation are not property owners in the way in which most single-family homeowners are. Most homeowners do not own homes simply to maximize a real estate investment. A homeowner *lives* in a home, manages it, and provides for its upkeep. Often improvements are made in the home that any competent real estate agent would agree would not return the investment if the house were sold. Indeed, this type of homeowner usually develops an attachment to the home. A house takes on a special meaning (a house is not a home). It is simply more than an investment. Frequently, this homeowner will not sell the home even when it is financially advantageous to do so. We know of people who have not sold their home for an astronomical profit despite the fact that it is literally surrounded by fast-food outlets. They wish to die in the home that has been such a part of their lives all these years.

This attitude is in sharp contrast to most stockholders who are indifferent absentee owners who will sell their stock whenever the price is right. Hence, all property ownership does not share the same characteristics. Surely a good case can be made for saying that most of the constraints should be on property that is held simply as a financial investment. Since the owner of such property has less incentive to take the same personal interest in managing, maintaining, and improving that corporate property, and indeed less interest in controlling its power, as is taken in his or her personal property, there is a greater case for the constraining of corporate property rights in the interests of society.

It seems clear that (1) property ownership is not an absolute right and that (2) property ownership comes in many forms. All types of property ownership ought to have some constraints placed upon it, and some types deserve special constraints. But what constraints?

One of the great issues in both ethics and in political philosophy is setting the criteria whereby my right to own and use my property must yield to the legitimate rights of others. But what are these constraints? In addressing this question we arrive at the third possible view of the relation of business to ethics. The primary responsibility of business is to make a profit, but there are ethical limits on what business can do.

THE RESPONSIBILITY OF BUSINESS INCLUDES MORE THAN PROFIT-MAKING

We concluded our analysis of the classical view of business by arguing that morality required that the right to pursue a profit could not be unlimited. All critics of the classical view agree that corporations have certain obligations in addition to making a profit. Some argue that the only additional obligation a corporation has is to avoid harm. Others argue that in addition to the obligation to avoid harm, corporations also have a duty to help solve social problems (duties of beneficence). Let us consider this position.

Maximal Account of the Social Responsibility of Business

To argue that companies have an obligation to help solve social problems is to subscribe to the maximalist theory of social responsibility. Here business is called upon to make contributions to society—to "do good" so to speak. But does this justify Sears giving to Sesame Street? Eleemosynary giving as Milton Friedman would call it?

What arguments can be given on behalf of these broad commitments to do good? Perhaps the most common is what may be called the argument from citizenship. Corporations are institutional members of society. Now surely if individual members of society have an obligation to improve society—to leave the world better than they found it—corporations also have this responsibility. After all, corporations, unlike individuals, were created by society. Corporations are citizens, and citizens have civic duties and responsibilities.

A second closely related argument is based on the duty of gratitude. Corporations benefit from society. On the basis of the commonly accepted principle that one owes debts of gratitude toward those who benefit us, the corporation has certain debts that it owes to society.

The final argument is that social responsibility arises from social power.[10] Great power is a gift, and it should be used to good ends. American business has thrived in this representative democracy and as a result has tremendous resources at its disposal. These resources should be used wisely to assist in solving social ills.

However, the obligations of the corporation to do good cannot be expanded without limit. What, then, does a corporate citizen owe to America? We all have duties as citizens, but these duties are not open-ended. The injunction to take social responsibilities into account and to assist in solving societal problems (where a corporation is competent) may make impossible demands on a corporation. At the practical level, it ignores the impact that such activities have on profit. At the theoretical level, it turns every action into a moral action and hence makes the moral life too demanding. A consequence of that is that if we ask too much of business we might get nothing.

But besides these arguments against business's responsibility to fulfill major social needs, there are others. First, who is going to define what social needs are and which get priority? If business begins to decide what social needs are good ones, that would mean that some executives who are in their position because their major forte is managing are now being asked to decide what are and what are not "worthy needs." Thus, utility-minded managers will be asked to make decisions that might not be best made by employing utility considerations.[11]

Second, business with its good intentions unduly influences social priorities that are best left to the government or the people's representatives. Government agents in principle are accountable to the citizens who elected them for the way they allocate resources. The business manager is accountable to no one. Thus, allocation of funds—the taking of profits away from the business or the stockholders—to fill social needs can be construed as taxation without representation. What recourse do minority stockholders have if they do not approve of the "cause" or "charity" to which their company is giving support?

Finally, the relation between ethics and business should be "realistic." As we have already mentioned, "pie in the sky" ideals or demands confuse obligations with actions that are above and beyond the call of duty. Such idealistic demands yield little or no results. For these reasons, it seems unwise to suggest that business has a moral responsibility to "do good."

Reformulating the Classical Model: The Obligation Not to Harm

To determine more precisely what the constraints on profit making are we will employ a modification of distinctions made by philosopher William Frankena, who has a somewhat different way of analyzing obligations.[12] He distinguishes obligations in ascending order of the difficulty of carrying them out: (1) avoiding harm, (2) preventing harm, and (3) doing good. Now it is possible that as the order of difficulty rises—that is, the more difficult the possible obligation—the less likely it is a strict duty or moral obligation, and the more likely it is merely a counsel of perfection, an ideal to be striven for but something highly unlikely to be achieved. This is important, because if the determination of the obligations of business is not grounded in some reasonable expectations of being obeyed—if it is too idealistic— the obligations will be dismissed as unreal and unreasonable. Further, if as the difficulty increases the obligation decreases, we may have a decision procedure for helping us sort out conflicts of duties. Thus, if a business had to decide to put in an anti-pollution device or fund *Sesame Street,* since the obligation to prevent harm is clearer than that to do good, the former course of action ought to take precedence.

To review, then, Frankena distinguishes among the following possible courses of action. First, *not harming*. Basically, no one has a right to visit harm on another unless there is a compelling, overriding moral reason to do so. Second, *preventing harm*. This is a less binding precept, to the extent that this obligation holds only at certain times. Finally, there is a prescription *to do good*. This is generally viewed as being "above and beyond the call of duty." Let us apply these principles to business. It is worth noting that Friedman's examples are usually examples of business "doing good." He rarely, to our knowledge, wrestles with examples where the actions of business cause harm, and he does not consider the prevention of harm at all.

Thus, we will attempt to reformulate the classical model by saying that business, along with its function to make a profit, has three obligations: (1) to act in accordance with justice, (2) to cause no avoidable, unjustifiable harm, and (3) to prevent harm in certain conditions.

A way to determine whether or not a business contract is of a moral nature is to determine whether or not the contract violates what some writers in moral philosophy refer to as the *moral minimum*. Perhaps the best statement of this moral minimum is that of Simon, Powers, and Gunneman.

The distinction between negative injunctions and affirmative duties is old, having roots in common law and equity jurisprudence. Here it is based on the premise that it is easier to specify and enjoin a civil wrong than to state what should be done. In the Ten Commandments, affirmative duties are spelled out only for one's relations with God and parents; for the more public relationships, we are given only the negative injunction: "Thou shalt not..." Similarly, the Bill of Rights contains only negative injunctions....

We do not mean to distinguish between negative injunctions and affirmative duties solely in the interests of analytical precision. The negative injunction to avoid and correct social injury threads its way through all morality. We call it a "moral minimum" implying that however one may choose to limit the concept of social responsibility, one cannot exclude this negative injunction. Although reasons may exist why certain persons or institutions cannot or should not be required to pursue moral or social good in all situations, there are many fewer reasons why one should be excused from the injunction against injuring others. Any citizen, individual or institutional [institution], may have competing obligations which could, under some circumstances, override this negative injunction. But these special circumstances do not wipe away the prima facie obligation to avoid harming others.[13]

A person's behavior is consistent with the moral minimum if it causes no avoidable harm to others. The notion of the moral minimum is easily contrasted with what we have seen as the moral ideal where one acts to produce the greatest good. A corporation morally need not surrender profits to produce the greatest social good. However, an argument can be made that it is morally required to surrender profits when corporate behavior violates the moral minimum (inflicts avoidable harm on others). Who would not argue that a corporation is required to surrender some profits by disposing of poisonous wastes in a safe manner, rather than saving the costs of disposal by dumping the wastes into the local water supply?

But defenders of the classical view might respond that there is no way to avoid harm. Production and distribution always involve risks and trade-offs. Every production involves some destruction. So proponents of the classical view will object that the condition is too strong. For example, they might argue that we know statistically that about 50,000 persons per year will die and that nearly 250,000 others will be seriously injured in automobile accidents in the United States alone. Such death and injury, which is harmful, is avoidable. If that is the case, doesn't the avoidable-harm criterion require that the production of auto-mobiles for profit cease?

Not really. What such arguments point out is that some refinement of the moral-minimum standard needs to take place. Take the automobile example. The automobile is itself a good producing instrument. The advantages it carries with it "justify" the possible risks that go in using it, just as the advantages that come from making paper "justify" (up to a point) the diseconomies of pollution. The good justifies at least some harm. Notice, though, that even classical theorists would not justify the existence of a company that produces heroin for general consumption. Heroin is desired, but it is seen to have no redeeming social value, only harm-producing capabilities. This is why there are some "industries" that are forbidden by law, such as selling my services as a contract killer. It may also be behind the prohibition of prostitution.

Society does accept many types of avoidable harm. We take certain risks—ride in planes, build bridges, and mine coal—to pursue certain goals. As long as the risks are known, it is not wrong that some avoidable harm be permitted so that other social and individual goals can be achieved. The avoidable-harm criterion needs some sharpening.

Using the automobile as a paradigm, let us consider the necessary refinements for the "avoid harm" criterion. It is a fundamental principle of ethics that "ought" implies "can." That expression means that you can only be held morally responsible for events that are within your power. In the "ought-implies-can" principle, the overwhelming majority of highway deaths and injuries is not the responsibility of the automaker. Only those deaths and injuries attributable to unsafe automobile design can be attributed to the automaker.

The ought-implies-can principle can also be used to absolve the auto companies of responsibility for death and injury from safety defects that the automakers could not reasonably know existed; the company could not be expected to do anything about them. Similarly, it is difficult to hold some companies responsible for pollution that they caused in the past when they were under the impression that their dumpings would be harmlessly washed away. In the 1950s, precious few people believed that industry was killing Lake Erie, or that DDT was harmful. On the other hand, few if any are ready to forgive the Ford Motor Company for not putting an $11 baffle behind the gas tank of the Pinto that the company knew could have prevented hundreds of injuries and deaths.

But does this mean that a company has an obligation to build a car as safe as it knows how? No. The standards for safety must leave the product's cost within the price range of the consumer ("ought implies can" again). Comments about engineering and equipment capability are obvious enough. But for a business, "capability" is also a function of profitability. A company that builds a maximally safe car at a cost that puts it at a competitive disadvantage and hence threatens its survival is building a safe car that lies beyond the *capability* of the company.

Critics of the automobile industry will express horror at these remarks, for by making capability a function of profitability, society will continue to have avoidable deaths and injuries. However, the situation is not as dire as the critics imagine. Certainly, capability should not be sacrificed completely so that profits can be maximized. The decision to build products that are cheaper in cost but are not maximally safe is a social decision that has widespread support. The arguments occur over the line between safety and cost. What we have is a classical trade-off situation. What is desired is some approximate mix between engineering safety and consumer demand. To say that there must be some mix between engineering safety and consumer demand is not to justify all the decisions made by the automobile companies. Ford Motor Company made a morally inappropriate choice in placing Pinto gas tanks where it did, because consumers were uninformed, Ford fought

THE MORAL RESPONSIBILITIES OF BUSINESS 37

government regulations and the record of the Pinto in rear end collisions was worse than competitors. Simply put, we can claim that if a company foresees that its activities are going to cause harm, it has a prima facie responsibility to avoid doing that, unless there is an overriding good reason not to. In the absence of a compelling reason to continue the project, the grounds that the project is profitable are insufficient justification and the profit-making enterprise should be scrapped.

But Simon, Powers, and Gunneman go further than simply prohibiting the inflicting of harm. They add an obligation to prevent harm. This moral responsibility can perhaps be seen by an example they use, the case of Kitty Genovese, viciously stabbed to death in New York City in 1964. Thirty-eight people either observed the attack or heard Kitty Genovese's screams without so much as calling the police. What was particularly shocking was that Kitty Genovese fought valiantly against her attacker and actually broke free on two occasions. Her opening scream was "Oh my God he stabbed me!" Her final shriek was "I'm dying, I'm dying." The time of the series of attacks was considerable; an early call to the police might have saved her. Hence, it may come as no surprise that society was morally outraged at those neighbors who stood by and did nothing. Clearly, even though they did not cause the harm, Kitty Genovese's neighbors had a responsibility to *prevent* the harm.

Are we ever "responsible" to prevent harm? Certainly. Consider if you are the only person passing a two-foot wading pool where a young child is drowning.[14] Do you have a responsibility to "prevent her death"? Of course. Most people would agree there is a responsibility to save the child even though one didn't cause the harm.

But under what conditions must we be "good samaritans"? Simon and his colleagues offer a list of conditions, which, when existing, place one under an obligation to prevent harm. Since "ought implies can" there must be capability. We have already seen that. But there must be three other conditions existing before one has a responsibility to prevent harm. There must be (1) a need, (2) proximity, and (3) one must be the last resort, that is, one becomes more responsible the less likely it is anyone else is going to intervene. Thus, if someone can prevent harm and he or she meets the conditions, that person has such a responsibility. One could argue that business, like human beings, has this responsibility to prevent such harm.

Let us look at a plant-closing case to see how these criteria can be applied. Does a company have an obligation not to close a plant under certain conditions? Consider the case of the Olin Corporation.

> Saltville is a small community of 2,500 located in rural southwest Virginia. Since 1892 it had been the epitome of the one-company town. By 1954, the original Mathieson Alkali Works had been taken over by the giant Olin Corporation. Although some of the symbols of the one-company town—for example, company houses and a company store—had become a thing of the past, the Olin Company was the foundation of Saltville's economic and psychological support.
> In 1960, Olin Corporation's Saltville facilities employed about 1,500 people. By 1970, that employment figure had dwindled to about 800. In 1970, Olin Corporation announced that it would close its soda ash facilities in Saltville. The closing would occur in a phaseout over a two-and-one-half-year period.

Presumably, a phaseout rather than an abrupt shutdown would give Olin's Saltville employees an opportunity to find other work.

In making its announcement, the company contended that three economic factors had led to its decision: (1) the failure of a 1968 modernization program of Olin's Saltville facilities to raise production, (2) the resulting rise in production costs as a result of the failure, and (3) stricter requirements by the Virginia Water Control Board that would require a $2 million expenditure at the Saltville facilities. Company officials placed most of the emphasis on the economic impact of the Virginia Water Control Board's decision.

Some were unconvinced that revised water pollution standards were the chief reason for the closing. In addition to the failure of the modernization program, the parent company had made a major error in the timing of its investment in aluminum production. Others focused on environmental issues. One study showed that Olin's Saltville facilities caused $2 million in damages per year to the river. Olin was in effect being asked to make total expenditures for pollution reduction equipment, which were equal to the damage it caused in one year. In any case, Olin never appealed the board's decision, and the state granted Olin a two-and-one-half-year exemption so that the shutdown of the Saltville facilities might be orderly.

The assumption that most people would not be out of work until mid-1972 was shattered in June 1971. It was announced that the soda ash facilities would close permanently July 1, 1971. Worsening economic factors represented by an inventory buildup were given as the cause. On November 18, 1971, Olin announced it would close its Saltville caustic soda plant on March 1, 1972. Increasing production costs and needed modernization costs were given as the reasons. The final blow fell when the Navy failed to renew a contract with an Olin Saltville hydrazine plant. Instead, the contract was given to another Olin company facility in Louisiana. Again, economic factors were cited. On June 30, 1972, all Olin facilities in Saltville were closed.

Despite the economic motivation for the closedowns, Olin took several steps to mitigate the charge that Saltville had been heartlessly sacrificed on the altar of profits. A generous severance plan and early retirement plan were implemented. Olin established a relocation assistance service. Olin donated plant, property and equipment to Saltville and contributed $600,000 to compensate for lost taxes and for planning and development. Some were unimpressed with Olin's generosity. The company "gifts" represented huge tax write-offs, and in any case did not fully compensate Saltville for the harms it suffered.[15]

Using the prevent-harm criteria, one might make a case that Olin had a responsibility to keep the plant open. Classical theory would argue that since Olin is a private corporation, and since the owners started it of their own free will, they are free to end it of their own free will. But if we consider the Simon, Powers, and Gunneman criteria, we recognize that our responsibilities are not that simple. Since we are all part of the same society, we have responsibilities toward one another. I may not have caused the girl being in the wading pool, I may not be a relative, but I am a fellow human in the area, (proximity), and proximity has to do with a network of relationships that exist. We will look at these shortly. At any rate, just as I am close by, so is Olin, and Olin's closing is going to cause social injury that could possibly be prevented. At any rate, Olin is proximate. The fact that there is going to be widespread unemployment and consequent hardship establishes a need for the people of Saltville to be helped.

This brings up capability. Is Olin capable? The Saltville plant is not showing a profit, but Olin is more capable of keeping Saltville afloat than would be the case if the Saltville plant were not part of a large company that arguably can afford some losing operations.

Finally, is Olin the last resort? The free enterprise system works well because of the freedom of movement of businesses, because one is free to move in and move out of businesses. Thus, it may be the case that it is better for the government to bail out or help the people of Saltville, and if the government can, the responsibility of Olin would be diminished, just as your responsibility to the drowning child would be diminished if the mother of the child were nearby, or the responsibility of Kitty Genovese's neighbors would be diminished or eliminated if the police were nearby. But if the police aren't and the mother isn't and the government isn't, then one person acting alone is the last resort, and the responsibility to prevent harm becomes more stringent. Consequently, we can argue that business may have not only an obligation or responsibility to avoid harm but also one to prevent it.

BUSINESS'S MYRIAD SOCIAL RELATIONSHIPS

Business has relationships to, and power over, all sorts of people other than stockholders, and thereby has the power to aid or abuse others. Hence, there are other relationships that involve moral responsibilities on the part of business. Thus, the classical model, which insists that business focus only on its responsibilities to its stockholders and concern itself exclusively with making a profit, is inadequate. But most of these obligations of fairness and justice will be clearer if we outline the various relationships that exist between business and the various elements of society. George Brenkert puts this point quite well when he describes the capitalist free enterprise system

> ...Each person participates in the system of free enterprise *both* as a worker/producer *and* as a consumer. The two roles interact; if the person could not consume he would not be able to work, and if there were no consumers there would be no work to be done. Even if a particular individual is only (what is ordinarily considered) a consumer, he or she plays a theoretically significant role in the competitive free enterprise system. The fairness of the system depends upon what access he or she has to information about goods and services on the market, the lack of coercion imposed on that person to buy goods, and the lack of arbitrary restrictions imposed by the market and/or government on his or her behavior.[16]

Thus we see that each of these relationships carries with it certain commitments and consequent responsibilities on both sides. After all, as Brenkert points out, business is not "them or us."

To begin, every business exists in a place and at some time. This may not seem too significant, but if there are rights that accrue because of something that happened in the past, then the fact that there were past agreements, promises, and understandings, both implicit and explicit, is a very important fact. Such past agreements create responsibilities.

The fact that business is in a place and is not some abstract ethereal entity means that it affects the surrounding environs, both environmentally, aesthetically, and economically. Businesses in the past depended on land and cities for a place to exist and for workers to provide the productive force. The business was like a young sapling; it may have been free to plant its roots where it did, but the freedom to pull up roots is not the same as the first freedom. The people in those places altered their lives to accommodate the business and began to depend on the business for their means of survival. A mutual dependency relationship based on space and time began to develop.

Obviously, the business in a place and time has a relationship to its owners, be they the stockholders or the individual entrepreneur who founded and runs his or her own business. This is the relationship that is privileged according to the classical view of the function of business.

Business also has a relationship with the consumers of its product. If there were no customers, there would be no consumers and no market and hence no business. To the extent that customers enter into free contractual arrangements with certain understandings with business sets up obligations of good faith, trust, and fairness in exchange; moreover, a host of other ethical relationships are established.

Business also has to relate to other businesses, the government, and its employees. Each one of these relationships carries with it a set of obligations that create problems. For example, place and time relationships leave business with the problems of how to handle pollution and what to do about plant closings. The relationship to the owner or stockholders raises the problem of how to justify the spending of money for charitable or not for profit purposes. The relationship with consumers raises problems of product safety and liability, and the relationship with potential customers brings up all the problems associated with advertising. Relationships with other businesses trigger a host of issues from industrial espionage to trade secrets. Employees make claims on businesses for fair wages, decent working conditions, compensation for injuries, and the right to a private life. There is also the relationship between business and government, which raises the questions about whether government regulations are good or necessary or simply unwarranted. One final relationship is that with the general public. This manifests itself in issues like affirmative action programs. Are these any concern of business? Should they be?

We have tried to summarize all these relationships in the following chart. (See p. 41.)

The various constituents to which businesses relate have recently been called "stakeholders." Though not owners of the business, they have a stake in what the business does. Proponents of a theory called the *stakeholder theory* would recognize that business has responsibilities to all its constituents. The term "stakeholder" was apparently coined in an internal memorandum at the Stanford Research Institute in 1963. It was defined as "those groups without whose support the organization would cease to exist." The list includes all of those we have mentioned. In the stakeholder theory, the function of business is held to be the harmonization of the interests of the various constituencies. The desires of each constituency need to be investigated and the best interests of each need to be fulfilled as much as possible.

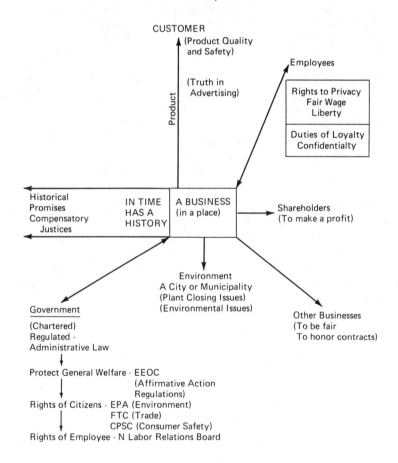

Business' Relations
and
The Ethical Concerns They Involve

CUSTOMER
(Product Quality
and Safety)

(Truth in
Advertising)

Product

Employees

Rights to Privacy
Fair Wage
Liberty

Duties of Loyalty
Confidentialty

Historical
Promises
Compensatory
Justices

IN TIME
HAS A
HISTORY

A BUSINESS
(in a place)

Shareholders
(To make a profit)

Environment
A City or Municipality
(Plant Closing Issues)
(Environmental Issues)

Government

(Chartered)
Regulated -
Administrative Law

Protect General Welfare - EEOC
(Affirmative Action
Regulations)
Rights of Citizens - EPA (Environment)
FTC (Trade)
CPSC (Consumer Safety)
Rights of Employee - N Labor Relations Board

Other Businesses
(To be fair
To honor contracts)

The purpose of business, according to the stakeholder theory, is to serve the interest of stakeholders. From this, two principles are seen to follow, at least according to Edward Freeman, one of the proponents of the theory.[17] The first principle is that

> The corporation should be managed for the benefit of its stakeholders: its customers, suppliers, owners, employees, and local communities. The rights of these groups must be ensured, and, further, the groups must participate, in some sense, in decisions that substantially affect their welfare.

The second principle holds that

> Management bears a fiduciary relationship to stakeholders and to the corporation as an abstract entity. It must act in the interests of the stakeholders as their agent, and it must act in the interests of the corporation to ensure the survival of the firm, safeguarding the long-term stakes of each group.

Under these principles, it is clear that corporations should be managed for the benefits of their stakeholders, and conflicts of interest between stakeholders and shareholders have a legitimacy under stakeholder theory that they lack under the classical theory. Still, it is not clear to what lengths the stakeholder theories would mandate that the corporation sacrifice profit and to what extent. If it includes "doing good" at the expense of the stockholders, then it seems to go too far. But if it takes account of the limitations that we saw need to be placed on doing good then we are probably in accord with stakeholder theory. What remains for us is to investigate the intricacies of these various relationships and spell out how they equate with moral responsibilities for business.

In the light of all that has been said, we suggest the following revision of the classical theory of business: "Business has a primary responsibility to make a profit, but in doing so cannot resort to coercion or fraud, and must respect the rights of all those who have a stake in the business, treating them justly and fairly, compensating for past injuries, doing no harm, and, where required, preventing harm."

SUMMARY

Let us review our progress thus far. In Chapter 1 we determined that the starting point for business ethics was with one's job description—in philosophical parlance with one's station and its duties. A person was responsible for fulfilling the obligations of one's role. However, we found that the job description had conflicts of duties inherent in it. Perhaps, it was suggested, we could resolve some of these conflicts if we examined the nature of the corporation to see what it was and whether it was a good thing. In this way we could see that business existed to make a profit, although not virtually unconstrained as Albert Carr would have it, and that this was a good thing according to classical theory. We then looked carefully at the criticisms of classical theory and suggested a modified principle of what the institution of business should be held responsible for.

We viewed the institution of business as a desirable way of improving economic well-being for most people. We presented a theory that opted for a profit maximization view *constrained by justice, and respect for individual rights that extended to all the constituencies of business that have a stake in the goings-on of business.* We saw that the respect for individual rights included at least the negative injunction that prohibited business from doing harm to its various constituencies and even included some affirmative duties such as preventing harm where possible and where this doesn't sacrifice something of comparable moral worth. We still need to look at the various practices of business, to see which of them are acceptable. We need to show in the next chapter why corporations should "be fair" by honoring others' moral rights. Further, we need to ask how the demands of justice and the avoidance of harm are to be carried out with respect to business's customers, employees, stockholders, fellow businesses, etc. What does the chief executive of a corporation do when interests of the workers conflict with the interests of society as a whole? Or when the interests of the local community conflict with the business? Or when the interests of the company conflict with an agreement or promise made to the chief executive of another company? These questions will be examined throughout this book. But before moving to them we need to investigate the moral presuppositions that underlie the very practices of business itself.

NOTES

[1]Albert Carr, "Is Business Bluffing Ethical?," *Harvard Business Review* 46 (January/February 1968): 145.

[2]Ibid., 145–146.

[3]Ibid., 148.

[4]Milton Friedman, "The Social Responsibility of Business Is to Increase Its Profits," *New York Times Magazine,* September 13, 1970, p. 126.

[5]Ibid., 33.

[6]204 Mich. 459, 170 N.W. 668, 3 A.L.R. 413. Majority opinion by Justice J. Ostrander, Supreme Court of Michigan, in T. Beauchamp and N. Bowie, *Ethical Theory and Business,* 3rd ed. (Englewood Cliffs, N.J.: Prentice Hall, 1988), 112.

[7]*A. P. Smith Manufacturing Co.* v. *Barlow, Atlantic Reporter* 97A 2d 186, p. 189.

[8]Robert Heilbroner, "Economics Without Power," A review of *The New Pelgrave: A Dictionary of Economics,* ed. John Eatwell, Murray Milgate, and Peter Newnan, in *The New York Review of Books,* March 3, 1988, p. 25.

[9]Ibid.

[10]Keith Davis and Robert L. Blomstrom, *Business and Society: Environment and Responsibility,* 3rd ed. (New York: McGraw-Hill, 1975), 50.

[11]Theodore Levitt, "The Dangers of Social Responsibility," *Harvard Business Review* 36 (September/October 1958): 41–50.

[12]William Frankena, *Ethics,* 2nd ed. (Englewood Cliffs, N.J.: Prentice-Hall, 1973), 47. Actually, Frankena has four principles of prima facie duty under the principle of beneficence: (1) One ought not to inflict evil or harm; (2) One ought to prevent evil or harm; (3) One ought to remove evil; (4) One ought to do or promote good.

[13]John G. Simon, Charles W. Powers, and Jon P. Gunneman, *The Ethical Investor: Universities and Corporate Responsibility* (New Haven, Conn.: Yale University Press, 1972), as quoted in Beauchamp and Bowie, *Ethical Theory and Business*, 2nd ed. (Englewood Cliffs, N.J.: Prentice Hall, 1983), 88.

[14]This example is adapted from Peter Singer, "Rich and Poor," in *Practical Ethics* (New York: Cambridge University Press, 1979), 168.

[15]This case is taken from Beauchamp and Bowie, *Ethical Theory and Business, 1st ed. (Englewood Cliffs, N.J.: Prentice Hall, 1979), 123–124.*

[16]George Brenkert, "Strict Products Liability and Compensatory Justice," in *Business Ethics: Readings and Cases in Corporate Morality,* eds. W. Michael Hoffman and Jennifer Mills Moore (New York: McGraw-Hill, 1984), 350.

[17]William M. Evan and R. Edward Freeman, "A Stakeholder Theory of the Modern Corporation: Kantian Capitalism," in Beauchamp and Bowie, *Ethical Theory and Business,* 3rd ed. (Englewood Cliffs, N.J.: Prentice Hall, 1988), 103.

Chapter Three

Morality in the Practice of Business

In the last chapter we tried to show that the institution or system of business was a justifiable system as long as its profit-making goal was subject to limitations of justice and fairness, just as healthy self-interest is justifiable as long as it is not at the expense of others. We also distinguished between the entire economic system and institution of business on the one hand, and the specific practices and activities that go on within business, such as buying, selling, marketing, hiring, firing, advertising, auditing, managing, making contracts, and such, on the other hand. We need now to examine those practices within the system, to see what if any ethical constraints need to govern them.

MORAL NORMS PRESUPPOSED BY BUSINESS

To begin, we will try to show that unless business adheres to a minimum standard of justice and fairness and gives recognition to the rights of those engaged in the practice of business, business practice becomes impossible. We will show why such practices as lying, stealing, fraud, and bribery are all immoral and why business practices themselves presuppose that such actions are immoral. We will then show that practices like advertising, hiring, auditing, producing, selling, etc., need to be guided by moral norms. Finally we will use moral norms to evaluate advertising and hiring practices.

KANT'S DEONTOLOGICAL THEORY

In Chapter 1, the term "deontological" was introduced to apply to a type of ethical approach. We shall adopt that viewpoint to show that practices such as lying and stealing are immoral. We will consider the position of the most distinguished deontologist, Immanuel Kant (1724–1804). Kant believed that morality, to be secure, must be grounded in something common to all men and women. His candidate was human reason as opposed to caprice or power. Two of his formulations of one fundamental law, which he called "the categorical imperative" can be put roughly as follows:

1. Act only according to that maxim by which you can, at the same time, will that it should become a universal law.
2. Act so as never to treat another human being merely as a means to an end.

Let's examine the two principles more closely.

Formula One: The Principle of Consistency

One way of viewing Kant's first formulation is as a principle of consistency of action. To understand what Kant is driving at, one should recall that familiar moral principle—the Golden Rule: Do unto others as you would have them do unto you. Kant's moral philosophy can be viewed as an extensive reworking of the Golden Rule, for to be willing to see an action universalized is to be willing to have what you are doing done unto you.

The Golden Rule makes people focus on how they want to be treated and then requires they treat others the same way. The reason for treating others the same way is found in the *principle of consistency*. In this context, it means that like cases should be treated alike. A few examples will illustrate not only the Golden Rule but also the argument underlying it.

Suppose that two teams are discussing the rules to be used for a pick-up baseball game. The pitcher for the Third Street Mud-Hens argues vehemently for keeping the traditional "three-strikes-and-you're-out rule." However, upon coming to bat, that very same pitcher now argues for four strikes. Isn't that pitcher guilty of inconsistency? Suppose that the pitcher replies that he is not inconsistent at all. When he agreed earlier to the three-strike rule, he was the pitcher. Now that he is the batter, the four-strike rule seems more appropriate. Such a reply would never do, but why not? Simply because we presume this person would not allow the opposing team's pitcher to change the rule? To make the point another way, would this person accept a rule in which people could change the rules of the game as they took different positions in the game? Again, presumably not.

To apply the analogy to moral problems, suppose that someone were to advocate discriminatory policies against Jews. To be consistent, that person would have to advocate discrimination even if that person should turn out to be Jewish. Presumably, he or she would not be willing to be treated discriminatorily; hence, as a matter of logical consistency, that individual cannot recommend discriminatory practices against Jews. Morality is not simply a matter of treating others as you would like them to treat you. It is also a matter of not treating others in ways that you would not like to be treated. This is sometimes called the *silver rule:* Don't do unto others as you wouldn't have them do unto you. Kant's point is that morality requires consistency of action and judgment when you are both on the receiving and giving end. Morality requires that you not make an exception of yourself, that you not engage in practices or follow rules that you could not recommend to everyone.

Kant has a worthy point. Sometimes this consistency requirement is captured by the notion of fairness: Some of the clearest cases of immoral behavior involve people trying to make an exception of themselves. One should not try to push into a line of people waiting to buy tickets to a popular movie. It is not fair. You wouldn't want it done to you. A student should not cheat on exams. It's not fair to the other students. A business executive should not engage in the practices of giving kickbacks and bribes. It makes the competition unfair. One should not break one's contracts while expecting others to abide by theirs. That is unfair. These practices involve making exceptions of oneself or exempting oneself from the rules without being willing to grant similar privileges to others.

But suppose that one were to reply to Kant as follows: "I don't care if other people try to take advantage of the rules by making exceptions of themselves. If they can get away with it, more power to them." In the business context, such a person would be willing to participate in a business environment where deception is expected. In situations like this, the Golden Rule fails us. Suppose that the way in which one wants to be treated is immoral in itself; suppose that one doesn't care if others try to deceive him or her. What would the Golden Rule say now?

Kant has a ready answer. Deceptive practices, besides being inconsistent, he argues, are self-defeating, in the sense that if the deceptive practice were universalized it would undermine the very social practices that made deception possible. Consider the question of cheating on exams. Suppose that a student were to reflect on whether it is permissible to cheat on an exam. If the student is consistent, he must agree to allow any student to cheat, for if he does not allow cheating by others, he is inconsistent. To be consistent, one must be willing to have the maxim of one's action be a universal law. Thus, this student must allow universal cheating. But if *all* the students were to cheat, the test would show nothing and the exam would not be counted. If the exam is not counted, the cheating is worthless. To universalize cheating is self-contradictory or self-defeating.

Kant's point is implicitly recognized by the business community when corporate officials despair of the immoral practices of corporations and denounce executives engaging in shady practices as *undermining* the business enterprise itself. A business community where cheating was the rule could not survive. A business community where no one trusted another would not be able to function.

Contracts and promises are essential in doing business. Let's examine these practices from Kant's perspective. When any deontologist enumerates the various relevant considerations that enter into determining what one ought or ought not to do, whether or not one has made a promise always appears on the list. Indeed, the notion of promise-keeping is central to moral thought. The injunction that one ought to keep one's promises is so solidly ingrained in both moral discourse and moral practice that it may be taken as one of the basic moral phenomena. Any ethical theory that cannot give an adequate account of this bedrock principle of morality is seriously deficient.

Kant's strategy is to show that if one contemplated breaking a promise, because keeping it was inconvenient or detrimental to oneself, such an action could not be consistently universalized. Consider this: If your reason for breaking a promise was that it was inconvenient for you, then your reason universalized would be, "Everyone should break a promise when it was inconvenient for them." But this is contradictory, for if anyone consistently recommended that everyone should break promises when it worked to his or her advantage, the very practice of making promises would be undermined. Promises, after all, are made because sometimes people want the security that something will be done or not done even if it turns out that such an action or inaction would *not* work to the advantage of one of the promisees. If such a universal practice developed, one could never make promises because no one would trust others to keep promises, and without trust that promises will be kept, making promises becomes impossible. Thus, there would be no point in making promises if everyone could break them when it was inconvenient or disadvantageous to keep the promise. In this way, any attempt to make promise breaking a universal law can be seen to be self-defeating.

Kant's point can be restated so that it applies specifically to business. There are many ways of making a promise. One of the more formal ways is by a contract. A contract is an agreement between two or more parties, usually enforceable by law, for the doing or not doing of some definite thing. The contract device is extremely useful in business. The hiring of employees, the use of credit, the ordering and supplying of goods, and the notion of warranty, to name but a few, all make use of the contract device. Indeed, the contract is such an important part of business operation that it is often overlooked. This is a serious blunder. Using a Kantian-type argument, we maintain that if contract breaking were universalized, then business practice would be impossible. If a participant in business were universally to advocate violating contracts, such advocacy would be self-defeating, just as the universal advocacy of cheating was seen to be self-defeating.

Business then requires moral behavior such as trust and keeping promises. Kenneth Boulding makes this exact point when he says that "without an integrative framework, exchange itself cannot develop, because exchange, even in its most primitive form, involves trust and credibility."[1] In business relations, trust and credibility are exhibited in promise keeping, especially in the honoring of contracts.

Let us consider for example a simple business transaction and move out to more complicated ones. In almost every case of a cash-for-product transaction, either the purchaser receives the goods before paying or the purchaser pays before receiving the goods. Seldom is the transfer simultaneous. Consider what would happen to business if, in an attempt to receive something for nothing, it was common practice for purchasers to claim that they had paid for the product or service when they had not. Or suppose the salesperson claimed that the customer had not paid when he or she had paid. If such behavior were universalized, ordinary commerce would become impossible. Even if such behavior merely became more common, ordinary commerce would become more time-consuming, more costly, and less efficient.

With the expansion of credit, the practice of cash-for-commodity purchases is diminishing. Credit arrangements enable the purchaser to possess the goods and services that he or she desires on the promise to pay for them later. But what if delinquencies and attempted fraud became universal?

Recently, some people have discovered that they must pay the family doctor directly rather than be billed. Upon inquiring about the reason for this new regulation, they were told that such a large number of people failed to pay their doctor bills that the doctor was forced to abandon credit. A more universal breakdown in credit would spell chaos for our market economy.

Kant's strategy was to show that, if one accepts certain practices, then certain sorts of behavior are self-defeating, since such behavior undermines the practice that has been accepted. In the preceding discussion we have shown how lying and cheating undercut the practice of making contracts, a practice essential to business. Such practices as lying and cheating cannot be universalized and, hence, from the Kantian perspective, lying and cheating by people in the business arena is as immoral as it is anywhere else.

Kant's strategy also enables us to provide an answer to the question of whether there are limits to the morality of my station and its duties. We now see that to accept the practice of business, one must also accept the universal moral obligations that business presupposes. But if that is the case, it follows that no role (station) within business could have as one of its requirements an obligation that went contrary to these universal moral rules. Such a role-related obligation would be self-defeating. Hence, duties required by role morality are always superseded by such universal moral requirements whenever role-related obligations are inconsistent with them.

A similar analysis can be given for such activities as theft, fraud, the use of kickbacks, and bribery. All such acts are acts of deception. If universalized, such deceptive activities would undermine the practice of business for the same reasons that the universalizing of contract breaking and lying would. Trust would be abandoned.

But let's develop this notion further. We have said above that people who are acting inconsistently in their own favor are unfair. Such a person is receiving the benefits of the rules against such activities without supporting the rules personally. Such a person is "freeloading." Most of us would characterize such freeloading as unfair or unjust, and as we saw, if such unfairness were practiced by everyone (made universal), business practice would be impossible. With respect to any kind of cooperative human activity, including business, the universalization of freeloading would be self-defeating. In this way we can establish that justice as fairness is a universal norm presupposed by business practice.

The contemporary ethicist John Rawls makes this case against the freeloader. Rawls asks us to consider an individual who voluntarily participates in a social institution and thereby accepts its rules and regulations. Presumably, these rules work out to the long-run benefit of those participating in the institution or at least are likely to do so. Otherwise, the person would not voluntarily participate in the institution. However, one who accepts the benefits of an institution, including the benefits derived when others participating in the institution follow the rules and regulations, but who himself or herself does not play by the rules, is unfair. He or she is a freeloader—one who accepts the benefits without paying any of the costs.

> In everyday life an individual, if he is so inclined, can sometimes win even greater benefits for himself by taking advantage of the cooperative efforts of others. Sufficiently many persons may be doing their share so that when special circumstances allow him not to contribute (perhaps his omissions will not be found out), he gets the best of both worlds....[2]

But, Rawls points out, this freeloading has a further psychological consequence. The freeloader's *sense* of justice gets undermined as does the sense of justice of all those in business.

> We cannot preserve a sense of justice and all that this implies while at the same time holding ourselves ready to act unjustly should doing so promise some personal advantage.[3]

Thus, aside from "being" unfair, a business person who is inclined to take unfair advantage of another will lose his or her sense of fairness. If more and more people adopt this system, the collapse of the system becomes more and more likely.

Since this is so, we ought to recognize that for a business person to assert cynically that business is without ethics is either unenlightened, irresponsible, and/or undermines his or her very credibility and possibly the enterprise itself. It is irresponsible behavior.

We have now shown that business requires justice in the sense of fairness both for moral reasons and survival purposes. But does it require more? We turn now to Kant's second imperative.

The Second Kantian Imperative

We will use the second formulation of the categorical imperative to help establish another rule governing business practices, specifically, the rule that a corporation must not, as it pursues profit, deny legitimate individual rights. To develop this argument, we focus on the second formulation of the categorical imperative—"Act so as never to treat another human being merely as a means to an end"—a formulation that can be referred to as the *principle of respect for persons*. Because this principle is often overlooked or is violated in business practice, it is important to argue for its centrality at some length.

Kant recognizes that only human beings are capable of being motivated by the moral rules laid down by the categorical imperative. It is human beings that place values on other things; these other things have conditional value—that is, value they acquire only because they are useful for human action. Human beings themselves, on the other hand, have unconditional value—that is, value apart from any special uses or circumstances that confer value. Because all human beings have this unconditional value, it is always inappropriate to use another human being merely as a means to some end, as if the person had instrumental value only. Hence, Kant argues, you should always treat a human being or a person with unconditional value as an end and never treat a human being merely as a means toward your own ends. The reasoning used to establish the first formulation of the categorical imperative is appropriate here. All people look upon themselves as possessing unconditional value. If one is to avoid inconsistency, one must view all other human beings as possessors of unconditional value. To treat human beings as possessors of unconditional value, one must treat them with respect.

Kant's principle of respect for persons can be applied directly to business practice. A Kantian would take strong exception to the view that employees are to be treated like mere equipment in the production process. Human labor should never be treated like machinery, industrial plants, and capital, solely in accordance with economic laws for profit maximization. Any economic system that fails to recognize this distinction between human beings and other nonhuman factors of production is morally deficient. In this way, Kantian ethical theory provides a criticism of the classical theory of the nature of the corporation. In the classical view, human labor is treated exactly like the other nonhuman factors of production—human labor is a commodity to be evaluated only in terms of market factors, such as supply and demand, and hence is subject to Kant's criticism.

Kant's second formulation of the categorical imperative has another application. We can use the contract notion to establish the central thesis that business firms must admit that its stakeholders have certain rights. For example, purchases are implied contracts, wages involve contracts, agreements with towns are contractual as are deals with other businesses and warranties. We argue that the fact that business recognizes these constituencies as capable of making a contract entails that business firms must recognize their rights. The structure of the argument is as follows:

1. A person can enter a valid business contract only if the parties to the contract are responsible, autonomous adults.
2. If a person is a responsible, autonomous adult, then that person must view himself or herself as a moral agent and be viewed by others as a moral agent.
3. One can be a moral agent only if one has rights that he or she can press as claims against others.
4. Therefore, a person who enters a valid business contract is a person who has rights.
5. To recognize that one has rights is to recognize that other persons entering the business contract have rights as well.
6. Therefore, a person entering a valid business contract must recognize the rights claim of the other contractees.

Premise 1 above asserts that the promisers and promisees are persons who must be considered to be responsible autonomous agents. In other words, makers of contracts are free adults who can be held accountable for their actions. Generally speaking, contracts with children, mental defectives, and criminals are not binding. The ideal contract maker is a responsible autonomous adult.

Premise 2 exploits the conceptual relationship between being an autonomous and responsible individual and being a moral individual. In considering yourself as a responsible autonomous being, you must consider yourself to be a moral being—an agent who can make moral claims against others. After all, what must a person be like to be capable of being a moral agent? He or she must be a rational person capable of making his or her own choices and be willing to live by the consequences of the choices. In other words, a moral being is a rational autonomous agent—just the kind of being who is capable of entering into contracts. When you enter into a contract with another person, you are treating that person as a responsible autonomous contract maker. From the perspective of morality, parties to a contract are equals. Hence, arguing from a Kantian perspective, you must treat other contract makers in a similar way. You must recognize them as moral agents as well.

Premise 3 is the key to the argument. It asserts that one can be a moral agent only if he or she has rights that can be pressed as claims against others. The essential concepts in a defense of this premise are responsibility, dignity, and rights. A responsible being is someone who can make choices according to his or her own insights and is not under the control of others. He or she does not live simply for another. In other words, a responsible person is someone who has dignity and self-respect. But one has dignity and self-respect when one can assert oneself in the world. One can only have dignity and self-respect if one can say such things as, "I may be wrong, but I am entitled to express my opinion." "I will not change the research results because such behavior would violate the code of professional ethics that I have voluntarily adopted." "What I do on my free time is none of the company's business." In uttering these remarks, one is asserting rights claims, for rights are moral entitlements. What we are arguing is that a person must be a rights bearer if he or she is to be a moral agent in the complete sense. The following quotation captures our point exactly:

> Rights, we are suggesting, are fundamental moral commodities because they enable us to stand up on our own two feet, "to look others in the eye," and to feel in some fundamental way the equal of anyone. To think of oneself as the holder of rights is not to be unduly but properly proud, to have that minimal self-respect that is necessary to be worthy of the love and esteem of others. Conversely, to lack the concept of oneself as a rights bearer is to be bereft of a significant element of human dignity. Without such a concept, we could not view ourselves as beings entitled to be treated as not simply means but ends as well.[4]

Let us review the argument thus far. One can enter a valid business contract only if one is a responsible and autonomous adult. But a responsible and autonomous adult is the paradigm case of a moral agent. One can be a moral agent, however, only if one has rights that can be pressed against others. Therefore, a person who enters a valid business contract is a person who has rights (premise 4).

The remainder of the argument is rather simple. Premise 5 represents nothing more than the straightforward application of the moral principle of "universalizability." What counts as a reason in one case must count as a reason in relevantly similar cases. The argument for our conclusion (premise 6) that persons entering a business contract must recognize the rights claims of others is now established as both valid and sound. Because the relation between an employer and an employee is essentially a contractual one, the thesis that an employer must recognize that employees have certain rights has been established. Moreover, because the relation between a business and its customers is essentially contractual, the business person must recognize that the customer has certain rights. And we can go on down the list of the various stakeholders. They all have rights contingent on their contractual arrangements with the business firm.

If the arguments set forth in this chapter are successful, something fairly significant has been achieved. The view of those who argue that ethics is not central to business practice has been refuted. Indeed, using the Kantian perspective (a central tradition in ethics), we have maintained that ethics is essential to business practice. Moreover, the ethical concerns that are central are fundamental to our view of the responsibility of the corporation, namely a responsibility to make a profit constrained by justice and respect for individual rights that extends to all the constituencies of business that have a stake in the goings-on of the business.

APPLYING THE MORAL PRESUPPOSITIONS OF BUSINESS TO ADVERTISING AND HIRING

To make our principle clearer, we will attempt to show how this principle would rule over two different business practices, advertising and hiring. It is hoped that studying these two practices will show when and to what extent the free-market system itself requires that certain moral principles, such as those articulated by Kant, need to be employed.

Advertising

Advertising has developed into one of the most pervasive practices in business. A hundred years ago, advertising was limited to catalogues, classified ads, and some billboards. It has since burgeoned into a huge industry. Today, over $75 billion annually is spent on advertising in the United States.[5] Advertising is obviously a beneficial practice, for it informs potential customers of the availability of products and services that they may want or need, products and services about which they otherwise would not know. Moreover, in many cases advertising has the desirable side effect of lowering prices, for by bringing more people to a product it allows production of more units at optimal costs, thus making the units less expensive.

Further, it is helpful to remember that the majority of ads take place in print, in display advertising sections in newspapers and magazines, (ads run by supermarkets or department stores, for example). Such ads make us knowledgeable about what is available, and for how much, a practice which on balance is quite efficient. Think of the times you could comparative-shop for an appliance without leaving your living room. Advertising seems to be an acceptable instrument to promote business.

Since advertising as a practice has desirable consequences, where is the moral problem? The problem lies in the use of deception in advertising. In a competitive market, one firm can gain an advantage over competitors if it can persuade more people to buy its product rather than the competition's product. Thus, if an auto dealer wishes to sell a used car, it might persuade a buyer easier by advertising it as a "cream puff." Potential car buyers are either more willing to purchase an auto from the advertiser or pay more for it if the auto dealer can convince them it is a better car.

Deception is easy to condemn but it is hard to define. Not all falsehoods in advertising are deceptive. A Wonder Bread TV commercial that shows a young boy growing before one's eyes or the Isuzu car ads seem like harmless exaggerations.

Many argue that much of what critics call "deceptive advertising" is nothing more than harmless bluffing. They argue that the purpose of advertising is to sell a product, and to sell a product you must put a product in its best light, you must emphasize its good points, and you must exaggerate a bit. As long as this commercial context is understood, exaggeration, puffery, and hyperbole are not deceptive. The claim that one's product is the best or the use of other such superlatives doesn't seem to cause serious problems for anyone.

Jules Henry describes the philosophy guiding the commercial context as the *pecuniary philosophy*. In the pecuniary philosophy, there is something known as *pecuniary truth*. A pecuniary pseudotruth is a false statement made as if it were true, but not intended to be believed. "No proof is offered for a pecuniary truth and no one looks for it," He adds:

> No sane American would think that literally everybody is "talking about the new Starfire," that Alpine cigarettes literally "put the men in menthol smoking," or that a woman wearing a Distinction foundation garment becomes so beautiful that her sisters literally want to kill her.[6]

Of course, some criticize the entire commercial context and the so-called pecuniary philosophy that accompanies it. However, the critics should note that something like the pecuniary philosophy seems deeply embedded in human nature. Almost all of us try to sell ourselves. Whether searching for a job or searching for a mate, we engage in exaggeration, puffery, and hyperbole about ourselves. And we expect others to do the same. We also use the pecuniary language to talk about our children, our jobs, our neighborhoods, or our spouses. Perhaps the world would be a better place if human beings could avoid hyperbole or puffery. But since such a change in human nature is unlikely, perhaps it would be more realistic to accept the pecuniary philosophy as operative in the commercial context, as well as elsewhere, and to discuss various rules or principles that might constrain pecuniary philosophy.

All of this notwithstanding, cases of genuine deception in advertising abound. Perdue Farm's implication that its yellow chickens were a healthier product than were Holly Farm's white chickens—since it seriously hurt the marketability of

Holly Farm's whiter chickens—seems more serious than harmless exaggeration. Perdue knew that the yellow appearance of its chickens was the result of the chemical xanthophyll in the chicken feed, and that it added nothing to the nutritional value of the chicken.[7]

In many ads, language changes its meaning. In life insurance ads, "noncancellable" and "guaranteed renewable" have technical meanings not at all what one would expect. Often age stipulations are thrown in. The physical world is subject to optical illusions that the advertiser can exploit, and psychologists study human preferences. For example, marketing research has shown that, if shoppers are given the choice between two boxes of cereal, one short and squat and the other tall and narrow, they will almost invariably choose the tall and narrow box, even if it contains less and costs more. Boxes and bottles are often much larger than needed for the quantity of material they hold. Testimonials, until recently, were also under attack. And so it goes. To many, these practices indicate that advertising, because it seeks to manipulate customer's choices, is an inherently deceptive, suspect practice.

It seems the dispute can be summed up thus. Deception is not serious because most people understand "the commercial context," "the rules of the game," or "the pecuniary philosophy," and if people expect to be deceived, as Kant observed, it is difficult to deceive them. Thus, the bluffing, the putting one's best foot forward, is both natural and harmless. Yet the other side points out that those who are most gullible, and hence probably most vulnerable (those like children, the naive, and the poor or sick) are precisely those *who don't understand the context*. In fact, then they are deceived and "used."

With these thoughts in mind, we need some criteria to distinguish the relatively harmless cases of puffery from the deceptions. To assist in developing these criteria, we need to consider exactly what is wrong with deception. People deceive others to get them to act in a certain way. Thus, we tell a lie in order to influence the behavior of others. A child lies to her parents so the parents won't punish her. But the fact that deception gets someone to act in a certain way is not the major problem with lying. What is seriously wrong with lying is that it vitiates the free choice of one of the two people interacting. One person acts toward another in a way she wouldn't choose to act if the truth were known.

In deceptive advertising, the deceptive advertiser is trying to get someone to negotiate out of ignorance or on false grounds. Buyers don't get what they think they are buying. This clearly violates Kant's *respect for persons* principle, for the deceiver is using others rather than treating them as autonomous agents entitled to make a rational choice. Deceptive advertising also violates the "universalizability" rule, either because the person would not choose to be given false information, or because universal deception would undermine any advertising. But we will return to this consideration later. Finally, deceptive advertising is harmful because it involves manipulation, which is to be distinguished from persuasion. The manipulation of emotions would involve trying to sell something by appealing to unwarranted fears or sex drives or some such tactic. Manipulation of the mind would involve giving false reasons for buying something.

Armed with knowledge of what is wrong with deceptive advertising, let us initially define deceptive advertising as a practice involving the use of false statements or inaccurate depictions of a product that are relevant to the consumer's decision to purchase and that are undertaken intentionally to mislead rational consumers.

This definition gives us two sets of criteria that allow us to separate deceptive advertising from harmless puffery, namely (1) depictions relevant to the decision to purchase, and (2) depictions undertaken to mislead rational consumers.

What factors are relevant to the decision to purchase? Three factors seem important: cost, amount, and quality. There are a number of questionable practices with respect to *cost*. Marketers in catalogues use something called *manufacturer's suggested price*. This manufacturer's price is then compared to the price the customer will actually pay. The manufacturer's suggested price is often an invention of the seller, concocted to impress prospective buyers with what a good bargain they are getting. At other times the buyer is only told the cost of the item based on a monthly basis, so that it looks more affordable than it is. Finally, there are even practices where customers are told they are being given an item free but that they pay only a small fee for services. Several years ago, a certain encyclopedia was being marketed door to door. The opening line of the sale was that the encyclopedia was a promotional gift. All the "lucky" person had to do was to buy the yearbook service and the research service. The fact that the cost of those yearbooks ended up being several hundred dollars was hidden. Recently, sweepstakes winners were told they could have a luxurious set of luggage for only $50, which represented a small carrying fee, when the same set of luggage was available in stores for nearly the same price. These are just a few deceptions relating to cost.

A second factor relevant to the purchase is *amount*. Some question the deceptiveness of packaging techniques, such as beer mugs with false bottoms or cereal packages, where the purchaser seems to receive more than he or she gets. Thus, warnings are required to check the *contents* or weight of the package.

The final factor is *quality*. Notoriously deceptive ads have recently been exposed in both the diamond and fur businesses, not to mention the less notorious and less serious Perdue yellow chicken case. Thus, if an ad promises more, better, or at less cost than is the case, the advertising is deceptive. The FTC's ruling in the Rapid Shave court case points this out.

The Supreme Court decided in favor of a Federal Trade Commission (FTC) ruling that determined that Colgate-Palmolive's ad showing that Rapid Shave could soften a beard that had the toughness of sandpaper was *deceptive*. The television commercial showed someone shaving sandpaper that had been generously lathered with Rapid Shave. The FTC admitted that Rapid Shave could sufficiently soften sandpaper so that it could be shaved. However, the catch was that the sandpaper needed to soak in Rapid Shave for approximately 80 minutes before it could be shaved. On the basis of this, the FTC declared the ad deceptive because the television viewer was deceived into believing that the actual experiment was being shown; the viewer was not informed about the 80-minute soaking. This would lead the viewer to believe Rapid Shave had a quality it did not possess.

Colgate-Palmolive disagreed that there was any deception. It compared its own "experiment" with the use of mashed potatoes instead of ice cream in all television ice cream ads. Just as the heat from the television lights made the use of ice cream impossible, so too the working time needed to soften the sandpaper made an actual experiment impossible. The court turned down the analogy on the grounds that the mashed potatoes prop was not being used for additional proof of the quality of the product, whereas the Rapid Shave commercial certainly was trying to provide additional proof.

We turn now to the second criterion for deceptive advertising, namely depictions "undertaken to mislead rational consumers." What counts as a rational consumer? The story is told of the woman who purchased Old Frothingslosh beer for a party. Old Frothingslosh is a beer that Iron City Brewery in Pittsburgh, in the spirit of levity, used to market at Christmastime, with the claim that "the foam is on the bottom." The woman bought the beer wanting to impress her friends at the party. The beer foamed where all beer foams—on top. The woman was mortified and thought of suing Iron City Brewery for false advertising, but her lawyer indicated she had no case.

The Federal Trade Commission in confronting this kind of issue has drawn a distinction between the rational consumer and the ignorant consumer. The ignorant consumer takes everything literally. He or she really does believe that, when Old Frothingslosh beer advertises that the foam will be on the bottom, it really will be on the bottom. The ignorant consumer does not show any common sense. It is generally agreed that to require business practice to be so open and literal that even the ignorant consumer would not be deceived would stifle business and seriously affect productivity. On that point, the conventional wisdom seems correct. However, the definition of the "rational consumer" is fairly amorphous. Sometimes, "rational consumer" is just a synonym for "average consumer." Advertisements, like television programs, would have to be aimed at those with the reading ability of a 12-year-old. At other times "rational consumer" is given a more normative definition. It is equated with what a consumer should know. The normative definition puts more responsibility on the consumer than does the definition that appeals to the average consumer. But what are the responsibilities of a consumer? When can a court say the consumer should have known better?

The criterion of *public openness* would maintain that a public practice is not deceptive when that business acknowledges the rules it is playing under. Ads for automobiles and real estate make it perfectly clear that the "asking price" is not the "real price." An ad for a home that says "Asking $120,000" virtually announces that the homeowner is in a mood to bargain. Auto ads for individual dealers stress the fact that they will match any other deal in town. They explicitly acknowledge the bargaining aspect of auto sales. Supermarket ads by and large contain none of this bargaining language. The price of oranges is not a function of an individual deal worked out between the individual purchaser and the supermarket.

Deception enters under the openness criterion when a business person announces that he or she is playing by one set of rules when in fact he or she is playing by another. Naturally, immorality also enters when one partner to a contract breaks his or her end. But as long as the rules of the game are known, then most people will accept consequences of business practices that they might not accept in other circumstances.

It is now clear how this discussion of advertising fits in with our larger analysis of the Kantian argument against lying. Remember, Kant argued that if the maxim behind a proposed action cannot be universalized, then the action ought not be done. An action cannot be universalized if its general practice would be self-defeating (for example, lying or cheating on exams). Suppose people believe that most ads are deceptive. In fact, a number of parents (including the authors) have taught their children to regard advertising as deceptive. Often, that type of teaching is not difficult. After eating three boxes of cereal so that one can send three box tops and 50 cents for a marvelous Star Wars toy, the toy almost never seems worth it. Children learn the lesson early. Jokes about used car salesmen are so ingrained in the public mind that honest used car ads just aren't taken seriously. Television advertisers are learning to their regret that consumers find the remote control "zapper" a useful device for avoiding ads by switching channels during commercials.

In summary, an ad is deceptive if it uses false statements or inaccurate depictions of a product that are relevant (in terms of cost, amount and quality) to the consumer's decision to purchase, and if the statements or depictions are undertaken intentionally to mislead rational consumers, where a rational consumer is one who operates in accordance with the publicly known rules of commerce.

This definition allows a fair amount of exaggeration and hyperbole in ads. Thus, the bluffing that goes on in used-car lots seems defensible because nearly everyone knows that asking prices are just that. However, even bluffing and exaggeration that are publicly known have their costs. What of the gullible, trusting, naive person? As a matter of fact, if *everyone* is aware of the bluffing or exaggeration that goes on, then it is no longer bluffing and exaggeration and it becomes pointless. The fact that advertisers still bluff and exaggerate seems to indicate that there are some gullible people out there still to be exploited. This ought to give us pause. At least some gullible people are deceived by "harmless exaggerations" and are thus harmed.

We have seen then that Kantian norms prescribe against lying and deceptive practices. The fact that some bluffing and lying goes on might explain why basically honest business persons feel frustrated and believe it is incumbent upon them to play the game. But the fact that unfairness occurs does not make it right; it just points out that the system needs to be more responsive to the claims of justice and fairness.

Hiring

At this point let us turn our attention to applying these deontological principles to the practice of hiring. From the classical point of view, the person hired should be the most qualified, for that would be the best market value. All other factors except those that increase profit are economically irrelevant. If there is hiring done for other reasons, then the hiring is not a market decision. Ironically, however, the initial principle governing hiring was not productivity or profit but liberty as it showed up in a practice called *employment at will.*

Patricia Werhane spells out the common-law principle of employment at will.[8] This principle states that in the absence of a specific contract or law, an employer may hire, fire, demote, or promote any employee (not covered by contract or law) when that employer wishes. The initial reasoning in defense of employment at will is easily seen. Suppose I start a small business. Am I not free to run it as I wish? If I have six employees, am I not also free to hire my nephew or a friend if I wish? Can I not threaten to close the business down if I don't get my way? It is difficult to argue such claims with the owner of a small business. One presumes the owner can hire a nephew who is not as qualified as someone else. After all, one need not go into business solely for profit motives. Perhaps this person wishes to go into business to provide jobs for family members. Nevertheless, as the nature of business changes, the liberty claim (the argument that "it is my business and I can do what I want with it") is less persuasive. As business becomes public in the sense that its stock is sold on the open market, or there are stockholders other than just the owner, the business needs to be operated in conformity with the primary principle—to make a profit. That means hiring the most qualified, in the sense of those who will serve the company best.

For example, if I am to be responsive to my fiduciary trust as a manager, I do no service to my stockholders if I hire a friend or even a family member who is significantly less qualified than another candidate to do the same job. The reason nepotism is frowned upon is that it encourages against attaining the best possible services in the name of friendship or familial loyalty. In short, *employment at will* seems to be incompatible with the goal of optimizing profits and productivity, a goal that is a primary consideration for any business person *as* business person. Of course, if it is my own company, and I set it up to provide jobs for my children, that is perfectly acceptable. But, note, in a publicly owned company, hiring at will is unacceptable.

We can, then, on the basis of what we have said, address racial or sexual discrimination in hiring. We can argue that in any hiring process there is no justification for discriminating against someone on the basis of race, sex, religion, or nationality, where those factors are irrelevant to the job. The irrelevance proviso is important, for one might insist that a woman's sex is relevant in the hiring of someone to supervise women's dressing rooms in a female boutique. But those types of necessary discriminations are not as common as one would think. It is even more difficult to see any relevant reason for discriminating on the basis of race. For example, even in the theatre, barring possible excessive insistence on realism, we could have and we have seen a black man play Henry Higgins in *My Fair Lady* and a white man play Othello. Thus, the recent discrimination against hiring blacks and women is as unethical as was the discrimination against hiring Irish or Italians in America at the turn of the century. Obviously, such a practice violates the "*universalizability*" criterion. Presuming one would not want to be discriminated against on irrelevant grounds oneself, people should not discriminate against others. Discrimination on irrelevant grounds also fails the *respect for persons* test for it treats some people as less than worthy of full consideration.

Discriminatory hiring practices seem to involve two things—some sort of favoritism, such as nepotism, and some sort of fear or hatred, such as racism or nationalistic bias. Both grounds are emotional, the former out of egoistic interests and the latter out of darker unreason.

But the debate about whether we can hire whomever we want or should hire the most qualified is not the most debated issue in hiring. The most hotly debated issue is that of *affirmative action*. In recent years, ever since passage of the civil rights acts, the government has seemed to interfere with both the employment-at-will doctrine and hiring the most qualified. It has done so through mandatory affirmative action in hiring. Because of government action, there are now legal requirements to be met in the matter of hiring. We will investigate these and the reasoning behind them and also ask the question whether there are moral requirements that bind businesses even when the requirements of the law don't.

Affirmative Action

What does affirmative action require? To begin, there are two types, weak and strong.[9] Weak affirmative action simply insists that available jobs be made public and accessible on an equal basis.

Weak affirmative action is justified as necessary for equal opportunity. But what does equal opportunity consist of? Does it only require announcing a job is open? Many argue that such announcements are not enough. In a competitive system, chances to succeed in the competition should be open to all; that is, one not only needs a chance to compete but one also needs to have a chance to win. Otherwise the competition is a *mock* competition.

To see what equal opportunity requires, let us look at what a competitive system with equal opportunity would look like. First, if competition is to be fair, then the competitors must have equal opportunity to compete. A race is hardly fair if one of the ten runners has a five-pound weight attached to each foot. Society should ensure that every person has a fair start. This view is captured by the *principle of equal opportunity*. The principle of equal opportunity is central to the American creed, and business practice should conform to it. According to the principle of equal opportunity, persons with the same ability and talents who expend roughly the same effort should have roughly the same prospects of success. Race, religion, sex, and family background should not be relevant to one's success or failure in the competitive struggle.

In thinking about what the principle of equal opportunity requires, however, difficult problems arise. These problems are now apparent as business struggles with affirmative action requirements. Let us consider a few of the more complex issues. We said earlier that if there is no chance to win, the competition is a mock competition. Consider the footrace example again. Although it is obviously unfair to place a five-pound weight on someone, we do accept certain inequalities as fair. There are height advantages and weight advantages in basketball. In the competitive struggle for a higher standard of living, society accepts inequalities in intelligence and talent, even though people impoverished in these respects are far less likely to succeed. What justifiable criteria exist for determining which disadvantages in the competitive struggle should be accepted and which ones should not be?

As a starting point, the following principles seem to reflect the thinking of many.

1. Natural differences among people should be accepted; differences imposed by society should not be accepted.
2. Disadvantages for which the individual is responsible should be accepted. Differences for which the individual is not responsible should not be accepted.

Under these principles, a footrace is not unfair if people differ in terms of weight or sobriety at the starting line. It is unfair if people impose penalties for one's color or religious preference. Thus, in hiring practices the fact that more intelligent people are more readily hired does not mean that hiring practices are unfair. To pay people in terms of the number of strawberries they pick is not unfair, even if some people are more adept at picking strawberries than others. A hiring practice is unfair, however, if blacks are systematically excluded. A salary policy is unfair if women doing the same work as men receive less pay.

Although most people agree that the two principles cited above reflect current policy concerning equal opportunity, it does not take much philosophical analysis to show that the principles are totally inadequate as they stand. First, the two principles are contradictory. If in fact individuals should only be held responsible for differences for which they are responsible (principle 2), then natural differences among persons should not be accepted (which contradicts principle 1). Second, principle 1 breaks the link between competition and justice. If natural differences like intelligence for which individuals are not responsible are allowed to count, how can the competitive process serve as a meritocratic allocative device? On balance, the least intelligent receive very little of the scarce goods and resources, but since they are not responsible for their lack of intelligence, on what grounds do they *deserve* receiving so little? Third, are any of the differences that are important in competition, and hence affect the results of competition, differences for which a person can be held responsible? Children who grow up in slums, who come from broken homes, and who go without adequate medical or educational resources cannot compete successfully. These children in turn produce more children who live in similar deprivation. This depressing cycle continues virtually unbroken from one generation to another. There is no way that most people from such backgrounds will be able to compete fairly for the economic prizes (goods and resources). Such an argument receives its most general and persuasive statement in the observation of John Rawls:

> Perhaps some will think that the person with greater natural endowments deserves those assets and the superior character that made their development possible. Because he is more worthy in this sense, he deserves the greater advantages that he could achieve with them. This view, however, is surely incorrect. It seems to be one of the fixed points of our considered

judgments that no one deserves his place in the distribution of native endowments, any more than one deserves one's initial starting place in society. The assertion that a man deserves the superior character that enables him to make the effort to cultivate his abilities is equally problematic; for his character depends in large part upon fortunate family and social circumstances for which he can claim no credit. The notion of desert seems not to apply to these cases. Thus the more advantaged representative man cannot say that he deserves and therefore has a right to a scheme of cooperation in which he is permitted to acquire benefits in ways that do not contribute to the welfare of others.[10]

If Rawls is right, many of the differences among people (for example, character) that have been seen as justifying the results of competitive allocation on meritocratic grounds can no longer do so. We cannot say that the lesser amount of goods and services received by the lazy person is something that he or she deserves.

Rawls's analysis raises some very disturbing questions since most of our social institutions (including economic ones) presuppose that people are basically autonomous and hence are responsible for what they do. The law has traditionally assumed that people are responsible for the contracts they make and, until recently, are also responsible for taking due care with the products they buy. You cannot blame the manufacturer of a power lawnmower if it is used to trim a hedge and the user cuts off a hand as result. However, recent laws requiring "cooling-off periods" before certain sales agreements become binding, the increased use of the concept of strict liability in negligence suits, and the advent of no-fault auto insurance settlements all reflect movement away from the view that people can and should be held responsible for what they do. If Rawls's analysis and recent practice that reflects it is correct, one of the central arguments for competition will be defeated. Competition cannot be viewed as a just-allocation device. People no longer deserve being winners or losers in the competitive struggle. How one fares is largely a matter of luck, not merit.

The debate over the extent of individual autonomy and responsibility is one of the central issues in contemporary philosophy. Whatever consensus develops, putting that consensus into practice throughout our social institutions will have important and wide-ranging consequences. These consequences will affect business practices as well. As of now, however, there is no consensus in the philosophical community or in society at large. Hence, one of the chief arguments for competition—namely, that competition rewards merit and hence promotes justice—is cast into doubt. That leaves the utilitarian argument as the chief basis of support. However, most people (including most utilitarians) cannot ignore the issue of distributive justice that arises in a society where competition holds such a central place. Our analysis of competition coincides with our analysis of the definition of the proper function of the corporation: If a competitive profit-motivated system of business can be justified on moral grounds, that justification will only be successful if the business community recognizes that it is the moral obligation of some other social institution to promote and put into effect programs that achieve distributive justice.

Even on the traditional criteria of equal opportunity, some groups have been discriminated against. What is to be done about those who have been discriminated against in the past? On the basis of past discrimination, should women and blacks receive special treatment now? Strong affirmative action programs have forced business to face this difficult issue. Under strong affirmative action a member of a certain class of people, a *disadvantaged* minority, is selected for a job over other candidates, because of membership in this minority class. This can be done in two cases. One is when all other things are equal. That is, given at least two equally qualified candidates for a job, the job preference will be given to a member of the disadvantaged minority group. More commonly, strong affirmative action will involve the following rule: Given two or more *qualified* candidates, the job will be given to a member of the disadvantaged group, even if that person is less qualified (Note: This does not permit "unqualified") than the candidates not belonging to a disadvantaged group.

There is a deontological justification for strong affirmative action in terms of compensatory justice. There was harm done in the past because of racial and/or sexist discrimination. Individuals from disadvantaged minority groups were hurt and consequently they should be recompensed. Besides this deontological argument there is the utilitarian argument that the integration of all groups into the society is an important goal, and thus preferential hiring is an effective means to their integration. We leave unsettled the equally utilitarian argument that preferential hiring is counterproductive because it causes more resentment, racial hatred, and strife than it alleviates.

Difficulties for strong affirmative action programs result because they are directed primarily at correcting harms caused a generation or more ago. In many cases, neither the perpetrators nor the victims of the harm are actually present.

It is a general principle of both the law and morality that some people should not be singled out for either benefits or burdens unless such benefits or burdens are merited. Job quotas and some other forms of reverse discrimination violate this fundamental principle.

Suppose that a corporation has deliberately discriminated against blacks from 1941 to 1960. Suppose that we could identify ten blacks per year who could have been hired but were not. At ten blacks per year for 20 years, we have 200 blacks who have been victims of discrimination. In 1960, one of the blacks sues and proves that the corporation discriminated. Suppose the court rules as follows:

1. The corporation must cease and desist in its discrimination. Beginning in 1961, qualified blacks will be hired.
2. The corporation must, in recompense for the 200 blacks denied jobs between 1941 and 1960, admit between the years 1961 and 1980 200 blacks who were less qualified for jobs under nonbiased criteria.

Let us assume that economic conditions require that those 200 blacks replace 200 whites who would have been hired. Although the first part of the decision surely seems correct, the second part of the decision is more problematic. The link that connects recompense to the injured party has been broken. The injury was suffered by the 200 blacks not hired between 1941 and 1960. The benefit is derived by 200 blacks who were less qualified for the job but nonetheless are hired between 1961 and 1980. The burdens are not carried by the 200 whites who were less qualified but nonetheless were admitted between 1941 and 1960. Rather, the burdens are carried by the 200 qualified whites denied jobs between 1961 and 1980. This seems wrong because equality before the law is being denied.

In response, it might be argued that the example ignores the secondary and tertiary effects of discrimination. In many cases of both proven and unproven discrimination, the original victims of slavery are dead, and the victims of Jim Crow laws are becoming fewer every year. But the legacy of discrimination lives on in the fact that many blacks are still disadvantaged and are denied equal opportunity. Indeed, this argument concerning the victims of discrimination can now be generalized to cover all victims of poverty whatever their race or sex. We now return to the issue raised by Rawls. Many of the victims of poverty are analogous to the footrace contestants with the five-pound weights strapped to their legs. Not to provide some way to overcome this handicap for such persons seems unfair. However, providing special consideration for such people in hiring and job promotion undercuts the economic and, hence, utilitarian advantages enumerated previously on behalf of competition. These advantages are maximized only if the most qualified are hired. In our example, this is not the case.

This discussion shows that society is rethinking what the principle of equal opportunity encompasses. When can we say that society has provided each participant a fair start? The elimination of prejudice and the establishment of a system of public education, which had been sufficient for the achievement of equality of opportunity in the past, are now recognized not to be sufficient. But no new consensus has emerged. Neither has any consensus emerged as to whether the burden (costs) for providing an expanded sense of equality of opportunity should fall on corporations (through hiring quotas) or on society as a whole (negative income tax, the federal government as the employer of last resort, etc.). However, this discussion does show that competition is certainly not fair in the absence of the traditional notion of what conditions must hold if equal opportunity is to be achieved. However, until some consensus reemerges on the criterion for what counts as equal opportunity, the rule of competition will not be completely acceptable to many Americans.

What then is the responsibility of business with respect to preferential hiring? We argued that business as business has no direct responsibility to "promote the general welfare," and thus no direct responsibility to resolve the evils of racism and sexism. Still, even though business has no moral responsibility to hire the disadvantaged, it seems we can argue that government which has the obligation to promote the general welfare and establish justice *can* oblige other subsystems, such as the business community and the educational system, to devote their considerable resources and power to alleviating social injustices. But that is an issue of normative political theory and beyond the purview of this book.

For the present, it is clear that for a business interested in maximizing profits, both the ethical and prudential requirement is to hire the most qualified person. At the very least, then, *not* hiring someone because of race or sex when the person can do the job is indefensible on both ethical and economic grounds. Moreover, when discussions of hiring and affirmative action come up, let us be cautious when we invoke the principle "hire the most qualified." That principle is an impeccable one in a society where there is true equality of opportunity. However, the first lesson one learns from job-placement counselors is to network. This reinforces and reflects on the old cliche, "It's not what you know, but who you know." We have seen clearly that that won't do as an ethical hiring principle, but for those of us in the mainstream of society, *whom* we know certainly provides a leg up. But that is a way of short-circuiting equality of opportunity.

Summary

In this chapter we have examined the practices of business and shown that they require basic moral norms, such as fairness, and justice. These moral norms are presupposed by any social practice in general and by business practice in particular. Immanuel Kant's ethical theory points out that the ground of these demands is the principle of consistency and the principle of respect for persons. We then looked at how these general rules could be applied to the practices of advertising and hiring. Specifically, what do the principles require with respect to truth in advertising and equality of opportunity in hiring?

In the next chapter we will examine how these ethical concerns show up in the various relationships that the contemporary manager is involved in.

Notes

[1]Kenneth E. Boulding, "The Basis of Value Judgments in Economics," in *Human Values and Economic Policy,* ed. Sidney Hook (New York: New York University Press, 1967), 68.

[2]John Rawls, *A Theory of Justice* (Cambridge, Mass.: Harvard University Press, 1971), 497, 569.

[3]ibid., 347.

[4]Norman E. Bowie and Robert L. Simon, *The Individual and the Political Order* (Englewood Cliffs, N.J.: Prentice-Hall, 1977), 78.

[5]U. S. Bureau of the Census, Statistical Abstract of the U.S. 1985, 105th ed. (Washington, D.C.: U.S. Government Printing Office, 1984), 548.

[6]Jules Henry, "Advertising as a Philosophical System," in Tom L. Beauchamp and Norman E. Bowie, eds., *Ethical Theory and Business,* 1st ed. (Englewood Cliffs, N.J.: Prentice-Hall, 1979), 470.

[7]Thomas Whiteside, "Annals of Business (Perdue's Advertising)," *The New Yorker,* July 6, 1987, pp. 39–56.

[8]Patricia H. Werhane, *Persons, Rights, & Corporations* (Englewood Cliffs, N.J.: Prentice-Hall, 1985), chapter 4.

[9]Thomas Nagel, "A Defense of Affirmative Action," in Tom L. Beauchamp and Norman E. Bowie, eds., *Ethical Theory and Business*, 3rd ed. (Englewood Cliffs, N.J.: Prentice-Hall, 1988), 345.

[10]John Rawls, *A Theory of Justice* (Cambridge, Mass.: Harvard University Press, 1971), 103–104.

Chapter Four

Moral Issues For Business Managers

We now see that while business has as its primary goal the making of a profit, that should not be its exclusive concern. Because any business develops relationships to various constituencies (that is, stakeholders) and because any relationship involves an ethical dimension, it follows that any business develops ethical responsibilities toward its stakeholders. But such a myriad of responsibilities creates conflicting duties or dilemmas for managers who run the business. For example, the responsibility to make a profit for the stockholders might conflict with the responsibility not to do harm to the local environment. Should a manager recommend a company be moved to another town for better profits, even if that means undue hardship for the current employees? We noted the possibility of such conflicts of duty, or role obligation, in Chapter 1. Now, however, we are in a better position to make some determinations as to the way such dilemmas might be resolved, or at least what sorts of moral reasons are relevant to the discussion. What we propose to do in this chapter is to analyze some representative ethical issues or ethical dilemmas faced by modern managers in their dealings with the various stakeholders.

But first a word of clarification. There are all sorts of positions in the business world besides managers—accountants, marketers, financiers, consultants, sales representatives, public relations officers, personnel officers, etc., and all run into conflicts of obligations in their work. For example, the accountant has an obligation to keep certain information confidential while at times being similarly obliged to report that information to the public. We could examine the ethical dimensions of any of the positions listed above. Our reasons for examining the ethical dilemmas of managers are twofold. In most corporate settings, the other personnel report to the manager, so the manager is the one with the responsibility for the overall running of the organization and is the one most responsible to the stockholders. Second, what will be true of the ethical responsibilities of the manager in many cases will be easily applicable to other positions.

Because every business impacts on its stockholders, its employees, its consumers, and the community it inhabits, in this chapter we will examine these relationships to see how and why the ethical dimensions of the relationship arise, and to what extent ethical considerations need to inform the practices of the manager.

Before we turn to those conflicts some possible misunderstandings need to be cleared up. In this chapter we consider ethical conflicts and dilemmas, not motivational conflicts. For example, if I as a manager am tempted not to deliver on a contract, or to cheat my wholesaler, this is not a conflict about what is morally right. In this case I know what is right. It's just that I am torn between doing what's right and doing what's easy or good for me but wrong and unethical. Being tempted to do the wrong thing is a phenomenon that has always been a human characteristic, but how to overcome temptation is more a motivational problem than a problem of knowing what is right. Thus, if we all agree that breaking a contract without a good reason is wrong, we have no ethical dispute, and there are many many areas in business ethics where there is no such dispute. Cheating, lying, manipulating, exploiting, etc., are wrong. The ethical conflicts that are the grist for the business ethics mill are those conflicts and dilemmas that arise because different courses of action each have good reasons to recommend them. In that case we have a genuine *ethical* dilemma.

Consider the following. A great deal of the time managers know what is the right thing to do, for if they can answer four questions about any action in the affirmative, there is no problem. The questions are: Is the action good for me? Is the action good for the company? Is the action good for everyone affected by it? Is the action fair and just? If the answer to all four questions is yes, the proposed action is the ethical course to follow. For example, suppose as a manager I propose giving my workers a raise. It looks beneficial to me and the company because in this situation it would elevate morale and hence productivity, which would reflect favorably on my management and on the company's profits. Certainly it would be beneficial to the workers and the community. That is an example of a happy choice where everyone benefits. If we reflect for a second, we realize that a good deal of business decisions are of that sort. If that were not the case, business would be in constant turmoil.

Nevertheless, occasions arise where what is good for me is not good for the company, or what is good for me and the company is not good for the broader community or the workers, and there are even situations, although they are quite rare, where what is good for me, the company, and the community of those affected is not fair or just. These are the occasions that provide moral dilemmas and moral problems.

Even here a distinction needs to be made. Sometimes what is good for the company hurts the community or is unfair or unjust. In those cases, to do what is good for the company is unethical. We know any number of executives who complain that their firms are at a disadvantage because they won't allow kick-backs or bribes or "perks" or some such activity. Such a complaint provides an informative example. Their line is usually to rail against the ethical standards. Yet, when pressed, they see that it is not the standards that are misguided but rather the unethical behavior such as the kickbacks or bribes. It's just that, because they have a healthy self-interest and wish to succeed in the competitive market, they don't like to have to work under a handicap. It is seen as unfair. Hence, they are *tempted* to take an unethical shortcut, all the while realizing and admitting that the original practice of kickbacks is wrong and has no place in business, and also admitting that if they did the same thing it would be wrong too. Thus, they don't approve of it as a universal practice, but they have a good reason for their doing it. "Everyone else does it and if they don't they will suffer unfairly," the argument goes. The unsavory activity is defended because their competition is engaging in unethical practices.

But even here the disagreement is not about what's ethical or unethical. The disagreement is about how to do what is good for oneself in a competitive market where others are taking *unfair* advantage (free-riding). Ethical business persons feel caught, because to do the fair or right thing will involve doing something that will harm themselves and their company, while to do what will help themselves and their company will involve acting unethically. That is a dilemma.

Nevertheless, even given this state of affairs, we should not be led into defending unethical actions simply because everyone does it. Everyone doesn't do it, and as we saw, if everyone did, business would self-destruct. Although we recognize the temptation to take shortcuts, particularly in an environment that seems to encourage it, and realize how hard it is to avoid temptation, we will still concentrate on genuine ethical dilemmas.

Our procedure will be to begin with the classical view of the responsibility of business and attempt to show how the obligation to make a profit gets broadened in modern times. To begin, we turn to the manager's relationship to the stockholders and ask this question: What obligations does a manager have to the stockholders?

OBLIGATIONS TO THE STOCKHOLDERS

Milton Friedman spells out what we take to be the classical position of the manager's relationship with and obligations to the stockholder.

> In a free-enterprise, private-property system, a corporate executive is an employee of the owners of the business. He has direct responsibility to his employers. *That responsibility is to conduct the business in accordance with their desires,* which generally will be to make as much money as possible while conforming to the basic rules of the society, both those embodied in law and those embodied in ethical custom....[T]he key point is that, in his capacity as a corporate executive, the *manager* is *the agent* of the individuals who *own* the corporation...and his primary responsibility is to them.[1]

Three Fiduciary Duties

It is clear that as an agent the manager needs to look out for the good of the stockholders. That is why it is *clearly* unethical for managers to agree to a takeover if it would enhance their position in a new company while being detrimental to the stockholders of the company for which they originally worked. It is clear that business cannot operate without agents, that managers are agents, and that they thus have fiduciary responsibilities that accompany their agency.

This duty is reinforced by the common law of agency that is applied not only to managers but to all employees and specifies three obligations: duties of obedience, confidentiality, and loyalty. While it is true that managers have special fiduciary duties depending on their rank in the corporation, it is also true that employees, because of their relation to the owners, have, in many cases, the same duties. We consider each of these common-law duties in turn.

The *duty of obedience* requires that the agent must obey all reasonable directions of the agent. The key term here is "reasonable." Clearly, it is unreasonable for a manager to demand that an employee exercise his or her skill on behalf of a personal interest of the manager; for example, having the company electrician work at the manager's house. These illegitimate demands are relatively rare. More common are orders to employees to take on tasks they weren't hired to do. In Chapter 1 we indicated the importance of a complete and accurate job description as a device for avoiding arguments about what one was hired to do.

Suppose, however, a manager and an employee agreed as to what the person was hired to do, but the employer ordered the employee to do something not in the job description. Would that constitute an unreasonable demand? In the interest of flexibility and efficiency, one might think such a demand would not be unreasonable. But we are well aware that women who have accepted jobs as management trainees have ended up doing basically secretarial work. On balance it seems to us that the job description should be viewed as part of one's employment contract and that manager demands that exceed the contract are unreasonable.

The *duty of confidentiality* is one of the three duties required of employees by the law of agency. Section 395 of the Restatement of Agency stipulates that the agent not use or communicate information

> confidentially given him by the principal or acquired by him during the course of or on account of his agency...to the injury of the principal, on his own account or on behalf of another...unless the information is a matter of general knowledge.[2]

This duty remains in force even when the employee leaves the firm and takes employment elsewhere. It extends to confidential communications and to all "information which the agent should know his principal would not care to have revealed to others."

Most often the duty of confidentiality is used to assure that employees don't betray their employer's trade secrets. An employee leaves with a wealth of experience at a *type* of job and often with considerable knowledge about a manufacturing process, a product, a computer program, research priorities, or detailed financial information. Some of this information can legitimately be described as a trade secret or the intellectual property of the company. For example, the formula for Coca-Cola is the property of the Coca-Cola Company. If an employee gave the formula to Pepsi, he or she would be giving away a trade secret. Other knowledge cannot be so constituted—for example, the general knowledge a researcher on computer technology at Bell Labs obtains in the process of doing his or her job.

Given the nature of a trade secret as *intellectual* property, a conflict of rights between the employer and the employee seems inevitable. The employer (corporation) has a right to its intellectual property; the employee has a right to seek gainful employment that uses his or her abilities. Moreover, the conflict between the right to the protection of property and the right to seek gainful employment does not exhaust the relevant issues. Trade secrets are necessary to protect American industry from foreign competitors and to improve productivity. They are also necessary if American firms are to undertake heavy expenditures for basic research.

The courts have tended to resolve these conflicts by insisting that specific information, like formulas or customer lists, is protected but that the general knowledge an employee attains on the job for all practical purposes belongs to the employee. However, even though the courts are now less restrictive, employees have an obligation to keep their employer's trade secrets confidential.

The final duty is the *duty of loyalty*. It primarily refers to the duty of the agent to avoid conflicts of interest that put the interest of the employee in competition with the interest of the employer. An employee can't set up a rival business or take for oneself a corporate opportunity. A corporate opportunity is a business opportunity that the corporation might take if its board of directors knew about it. If an employee receives information on a possible product that is in the corporation's domain, the employee must notify the corporation of its existence. Not to do so would deprive the corporation of a corporate opportunity. Consequently, if a manager has committed contractually or otherwise to a principal to perform certain services, then the manager is obliged to refrain from taking on other obligations that would conflict with that. To freely put oneself in a conflict situation is unethical.

Avoiding conflicts of interest involves more than an agent not competing with the principal. Some accountants have recently taken on the task of selling securities. Their work as accountants and auditors certainly gives them valuable information that would be of benefit to their clients who are seeking investment advice. But it unnecessarily puts them into a conflict-of-interest situation. Imagine the strain on objectivity if an accountant is auditing a company that some customers wish to invest in substantially. We have talked to accountants who think the ethical conduct standards of the National Association of Accountants restrict their freedom too much. But they miss the point. If an accountant is engaged as an agent for the public, there is an ethical obligation to *avoid* putting oneself into a situation where a potential conflict might come up.

What of those situations that arise when your obligation of loyalty to a principal conflicts with your obligation to others? Is the responsibility of the agent to the principal limited at all? Let us look further at what Friedman says:

> Of course, the corporate executive is also a person in his own right. As a person he may have many other responsibilities that he recognizes or assumes voluntarily—to his family, his conscience, his feelings of charity, his church, his clubs, his city, his country....He may refer to some of these responsibilities as "social responsibilities." But in these respects he is acting as a principal, not an agent.[3]

Friedman sees these responsibilities as social and hence recognizes them but still he does not suggest what one is to do when these conflicts arise.

An Exception to Fiduciary Duty: Whistle-Blowing

Up to now we have been concentrating on the manager's obligations to the stockholder and similarly the employee's obligations to the employer. Recently, though, public attention has focused on the obligation of an employee, or agent, not only to disobey the demands of the principal but also to report the wrongdoing of the principal—to blow the whistle.

Whether or not they are asked to participate in the act, employees are often in a position to know about the illegal or immoral actions of a supervisor or employer. Should an employee who is asked to participate in an illegal or immoral action, or who witnesses the illegal or immoral action of a supervisor or employer, inform the public? Whenever these questions are answered in the affirmative and the public is informed, we have cases of whistle-blowing. On a first account, whistle-blowing is the act by an employee of informing the public on the immoral or illegal behavior of an employer or supervisor.

One of the better-known cases in which whistle-blowers have lost their jobs is the BART case. BART is the acronym for the Bay Area Rapid Transit system, a modern rail transit system in San Francisco. During construction of the line, three engineers became deeply concerned over the safety of certain features of the system. Holger Hjortsvang reported, to no avail, his concerns about the Automatic Train Control System that was being built by the Westinghouse Corporation. Just a few months later, another engineer, Robert Bruder, became concerned about Westinghouse's lack of tests on certain equipment. Still later, Max Blankenzee, a senior programmer, joined Mr. Hjortsvang in sharing his concerns. Having received no response from various memoranda they had filed, the three engineers met with a member of the BART board of directors. Following the meeting, confidential memos shared with board member Daniel Helex appeared in the *Contra Costa Times*, and the report of a private consultant in support of the three engineers was ridiculed after being presented to the full board. Three days later all three engineers were fired. The engineers sued and each won $25,000 in an out-of-court settlement. It took from eight to fifteen months for the three engineers to find satisfactory jobs elsewhere. In addition to the economic stress, the psychological stress was relatively severe on all of them.

Despite the apparent injustice that results when whistle-blowers protect the public interest at great personal cost, many business people have little sympathy for them. According to these people, whistle-blowers have violated one of the chief duties of an employee—the duty to be loyal to one's employer. This attitude is perhaps best captured in remarks by James M. Roche, former president of General Motors.

> Some critics are now busy eroding another support of free enterprise—the loyalty of a management team, with its unifying values of cooperative work. Some of the enemies of business now encourage an employee to be disloyal to the enterprise. They want to create suspicion and disharmony, and pry into the proprietary interests of the business. However this is labeled—industrial espionage, whistle blowing, or professional responsibility—it is another tactic for spreading disunity and creating conflict.[4]

However, the obligation of loyalty as an overriding obligation has recently come under attack.[5] The general consensus seems to be that one has a duty to be loyal only if the object of loyalty is one that is morally appropriate.

One cannot assume, however, that the claims of all whistle-blowers are obviously true and that the denials of all employers are obviously false. Some whistle-blowers may be trying to seize more power within the company. BART made just such a charge against engineer Hjortsvang. Others try to create a whistle-blowing case for the purpose of covering up genuine personal inadequacies—inadequacies that represent the real reason for their being disciplined or dismissed. What is needed is a careful definition of whistle-blowing along with guidelines outlining what considerations should be taken into account to justify acts of whistle-blowing. To begin, let us define the whistle-blower:

> A whistle blower is an employee or officer of any institution, profit or non-profit, private or public, who believes either that he/she has been ordered to perform some act or he/she has obtained knowledge that the institution is engaged in activities which a) are believed to cause unnecessary harm to third parties, b) are in violation of human rights or c) run counter to the defined purpose of the institution and who inform the public of this fact.[6]

With respect to corporations, the discerning reader will note that the whistle-blower in business reports activities that violate either the basic moral presuppositions on which the business enterprise rests or that violate the purpose of the corporate enterprise. The theoretical structure presented in earlier chapters provides the conceptual apparatus for distinguishing whistle-blowing from tattling on the one hand and sabotage on the other.

What can be said on behalf of this definition? First, it limits the class of moral infractions that an employee should make public. A person who makes a point of informing on every indiscretion is a nuisance and is more appropriately an object of scorn rather than a subject of praise. Who wants to know every time someone utters an unkind word about one's supervisor or uses a piece of office stationery for a personal letter. Parents encourage their children not to tattle, and those in the business world should not be tattletales either. Whistle-blowing is reserved conceptually only for those serious moral faults spelled out in the definition. Of course, people who commit these relatively minor moral faults ought not to do them. An injunction against tattling does not make the actions of the perpetrators blameless. Rather, the injunction against tattling is based on the view that it is inappropriate for everyone to have as his or her responsibility the task of informing others of the minor moral faults of everyone else. Given the rancor and ill will that are caused when people do tattle, there are good utilitarian arguments against tattling. In addition, the definition limits the scope of one's response to immoral behavior. A whistle-blower's responsibility is limited to informing the public. The responsibility does not extend to taking any retaliatory action against the employer or firm. The concept of "whistle-blower" must be kept distinct from the concept of "saboteur."

To define the whistle-blower is not thereby to justify all acts of whistle-blowing. The definition of something is one thing: its justification is another. The following list of conditions, when met, provide sufficient grounds for an act of whistle-blowing:

1. The whistle-blowing is done from the appropriate moral motive—namely, as provided in the definition of whistle-blowing.
2. The whistle-blower, except in special circumstances, has exhausted all internal channels for dissent before informing the public.
3. The whistle-blower has made certain that his or her belief that inappropriate actions are ordered or have occurred is based on evidence that would persuade a reasonable person.
4. The whistle-blower has acted after a careful analysis of the danger: (a) how serious is the moral violation? (b) how immediate is the moral violation? (c) is the moral violation one that can be specified?
5. The whistle-blower's action is commensurate with one's responsibility for avoiding and/or exposing moral violations.
6. The whistle-blowing has some chance of success.

This list of justifying conditions deserves some comment. The question of motive is extremely important. Since whistle-blowing does violate a prima facie duty of loyalty to one's employer, whistle-blowing must be based on moral grounds if it is to be justified. The moral aim of whistle-blowing is deemed so central that it is made part of the definition—namely, whistle-blowing aims at exposing unnecessary harm, violations of human rights, or conduct counter to the defined purpose of the corporation. However, the moral dimensions of whistle-blowing are not exhausted by examining its aim. Many moral philosophers have insisted that consideration of motives is relevant in assessing the morality of a person's action. Suppose that a potential assassin attempts to push the President of the United States in front of a train. As the President stumbles, another assassin (whose existence is unknown to the first) fires a shot that misses the President. Surely the action of the first potential assassin is not morally justified even though the act had good results.

Now consider possible motives for whistle-blowing. A desire to attract attention, to get ahead, to shift the focus away from one's genuine weakness, and a general propensity toward being a troublemaker all represent possible motives for whistle-blowing, but obviously none of them passes the first justificatory test. A whistle-blower's motive should be to protect the public interest. Anything less than that undercuts the justification of whistle-blowing.

Yet another justificatory constraint is that the whistle-blower exhaust all internal channels for dissent. Because the whistle-blower does have some obligations to the employer, he or she should—at least in normal circumstances—use the institutional mechanisms that have been created for the purpose of registering dissent with the policies or actions of the corporation. One can be cynical about such institutional mechanisms, but, as we will see in the next chapter, such self-regulating mechanisms are desirable. In fact, two contemporary theorists have argued that

> The task of ethical management is to have anticipated the pressures which would give rise to the concealed and harmful practice, and to have helped create patterns of communication within the organization so that whistle blowing would not be necessary. The focus on attempting to assure protection for the whistle blower is, from the point of view of managerial ethics, basically misconceived—the managerial task is to prevent the necessity of whistle blowing.[7]

As such effective mechanisms develop, the whistle-blower is under an obligation to use them.

Yet another element in justified whistle-blowing refers to the evidential base on which the whistle-blowing is done. Charges of immorality should be based on strong evidence. Definitions of what counts as strong evidence go far beyond the subject matter of this book. We rest content with the semilegal notion that the evidence should be strong enough so that any person in a similar situation would be convinced that the practice being protested is indeed immoral. We have already seen how the concept of the reasonable consumer functions in judgments of deceptive advertising. The reasonable consumer standard is also used in liability and negligence lawsuits; hence, we will let the concept suffice here.

Still another requirement for justified whistle-blowing focuses on the nature of the moral violation itself. First, the seriousness of the violation should be considered. Just as parents should only call the doctor when their child is seriously ill and not when the illnesses are minor, whistle-blowers should only inform on their employers for grave moral matters. Fastidiousness about moral matters is not a requirement for business ethics. Another element to be considered is how immediate the moral violation is. The greater the time before the violation is to occur, the greater the chances that internal mechanisms will prevent the anticipated violation. In general, whistle-blowing is more justified the more immediate the violation is. Finally, the violation should be something specific. General claims about a rapacious company, obscene profits, and actions contrary to the public interest simply will not do. Such claims must be backed up with identifiable examples— examples that will stand up under the other justificatory tests.

Still another justificatory requirement enables us to return to the discussion of role morality in Chapter 1. Some positions within the corporate structure have as part of the job description a concern with the morality of corporate actions. Some jobs such as ombudsman or vice-president for corporate responsibility are defined as being concerned with corporate moral behavior. In other cases, certain kinds of moral activities are the responsibilities of corporate personnel. Corporate auditors check the legitimacy of expense account statements. Quality control personnel have special responsibilities concerning consumer safety. When some moral matter is the specific assignment of an employee, that person has special responsibilities associated with that role. When the corporate role gives an employee explicit responsibility for some matter with ethical dimensions, the corporation is normally committed to following the advice of the person given the responsibility. After all, failure to do so would create a serious ethical dilemma for the employee with the moral responsibility. If the corporation overruled the advice, the employee would either have to acquiesce in an activity that he or she has already determined to be illegal or immoral or he or she would have to blow the whistle.

However, responsibilities for moral matters are not limited to job descriptions created by the business institutions themselves. Where corporations make use of *professional* employees, there are certain moral obligations associated with the role of that profession. Often those obligations are spelled out in a professional code of ethics. The best-known examples are in engineering and accounting. One provision of the code of the American Society of Civil Engineers is that an engineer "will use his knowledge and skill for the advancement of human welfare and refuse any assignment contrary to this good." The National Society of Professional Engineers has a rather extensive code of ethics consisting of 15 major sections. The National Association of Accountants also has a professional code of ethics, which among its admonitions requires that accountants "refrain from engaging in any activity that would prejudice their ability to carry out their duties ethically." Being a professional engineer or accountant binds those engineers and accountants to the code of conduct of the society and by implication binds the companies that employ these individuals as well. After all, in hiring a professional it is presumed that one wishes to employ someone who meets certain professional standards, and, unless specified otherwise, an employer accepts all the standards of professional behavior associated with that profession.

The final justificatory condition is more controversial. It requires that the whistle-blowing have some chance of success. If there is no hope in arousing societal or government pressure, then one is needlessly exposing oneself and one's loved ones to hardship for no conceivable moral gain. It is not simply a matter of saying that an employee is not obligated to blow the whistle if there is no chance of success, but that whistle-blowing that does not have a chance of success is less justified, all things being equal, than is whistle-blowing that does have a chance of success. The reader should note that we are not saying that such whistle-blowing is never justified and hence should never be done. Sometimes such whistle-blowing should be done if, for example, the violation is especially grave and the whistle-blower's other personal obligations are few. On balance, however, given the dangers that personal whistle-blowers run, the more likely the chances of success, the more justified the act of whistle-blowing is. So much for the obligation to blow the whistle.

In summarizing this section on the responsibility of the agent to the stockholders, we have seen that although Friedmanians want the manager to be a loyal agent and emphasize his or her responsibility to maximize profits, there are some questions about the limits of this responsibility. We have already shown that business has other responsibilities besides *simply* making a profit, and indeed Friedman makes room for these when he adds "without force and fraud"...and..."while conforming to the basic rules of society, both those embodied in law and those embodied in ethical custom." Given these limitations, how much does an agent owe to the company? The answer seems to be emerging that the agent is obliged to look out for the best interests of the principal (manager), who in turn is obligated to look out for the best interests of the company to the extent that this is in conformity with moral requirements.

As we mentioned above, ethical problems and dilemmas arise only when conflicting demands arise. Absent any conflict, the agent should do what the principal wishes. But in business matters, the conflict usually arises when the requirements of profit-making conflict with the needs of those other than the owners or stockholders. The "loyal" agent/manager faces problems and dilemmas when the profit-making interests of the firm conflict with the interests of the other stakeholders.

We turn now to an examination of when those interests of other stakeholders can legitimately override the interests of the stockholders. As we said, we will look at the interests of three groups of stakeholders: the community where the business is located, the customers of the business, and the employees of the business. We turn to the relationship of a business to its community, to see what moral obligations arise from that relationship.

OBLIGATIONS TO THE COMMUNITY

What obligations, if any, does a company and hence its managers have toward the community in which it is located? How much should managers temper their profit-maximizing decisions because of claims made on the business by the local community?

Obligations to a community, viewing the community as a stakeholder, is a relatively new perspective. Under a laissez-faire model of business, there were relatively few ethical claims that a community would press against a business. After all, since the decision to start a business was the free decision of the entrepreneur, is not the decision to close it down, move it, or abandon it also the free decision of the owner? Is the owner not free to do with the business what he or she wishes? What he or she wants?

Recently, this argument defending the freedom of the owner has been challenged. It makes no sense for a community to *allow* a business or owner to set up shop in the midst of the community unless such an enterprise will benefit the community. Thus, a business when it starts is presumed to be in the interests of both the owners and the community in which it is established. Its existence rests on at least an implied agreement or contract that this relationship will be mutually beneficial. Although neither party can foresee all possible future harm, one could argue that there is at least an implicit understanding that any harm accruing to either partner—the business or the community—be avoided if at all possible. We will adopt this view of the relationship and use it as a basis for the discussion of two types of conflicts between a business and its community—plant closings and environmental pollution.

To begin, we maintain that the relationship between a business and its community involves at least three ethical principles:

1. Neither party should harm the other without sufficient reason. (Do no harm)
2. Compensation ought to be made for past harms or costs. (Compensatory justice)
3. In some instances, business might be obliged to prevent harm. (Obligation to prevent harm)

Plant Closings

To show the application of these principles, let us turn to an example of a plant closing, the Black and Decker factory in Allentown, Pennsylvania.

In April of 1984 Black and Decker bought General Electric's houseware division for three hundred million dollars. Part of that purchase included G.E.'s Allentown plant. The plant had been turning out kitchenware since 1946. Workers claimed the Allentown plant had been operating in the black, a contention the company did not dispute. On November 8, 1984 Black and Decker announced that the Allentown plant was being closed because it was one of the firm's most "vertically integrated" plants, and because it was one of three B&D factories being shut down after the G.E. acquisition, in order to eliminate excess production capacity company wide. Seven plants in G.E.'s appliance division were operating at just 50% capacity.

The 870 workers being put out of work felt a sense of betrayal as did the city of Allentown. The plant was an integral part of Allentown since 1946, and had operated at a profit. Six months before the closure announcement the workers were told that they were doing a good job, and negotiated a 16-month extension of their contract with G.E. These workers averaged 23 years of service with G.E. Union Local 128 president Kokolus said, "I think they made a big mistake. They betrayed not only us, but the people of Allentown."

Under the plant-closure provisions negotiated in the previous G.E. contract, the majority of the plant workers are expected to get an $18,000 lump payment and one year's medical benefits, as well as entitlement to $1,800 for job retraining. However, at the time unemployment in Allentown was 8.8% as compared to 7.2% nationally and was expected to rise even more since 1,000 workers were being laid off by the Mack Truck company in Allentown.[8]

Even if the move to close the Black and Decker plant makes "economic sense" there is a question of whether it is ethically justified, or was Black and Decker's action an immoral "betrayal"? We don't propose to solve the issue, but as a case study it raises interesting questions and we will suggest possible ways the three ethical principles can be applied to the situation. Aside from the general question of a plant closing, the case also raises the question of what is owed to employees of one company when that company is taken over by another. Does the company acquire the obligations of the company purchased as well as the assets? If not, why not? We will pass over this question.

Generally, two arguments are made in support of the right of an owner to close a plant at will: (1) The right to close or move a plant is defended on the grounds that one can do what one wants with one's property, and (2) the profitability argument that defends the rights of owners to do what they want to maximize profits as long as that does not involve force or fraud.

We turn to the first argument. As we saw in Chapter 2, an owner often uses the appeal to freedom. Our free-market system is such that no one should be coerced. I am free to start a business and make a product, and people are free to buy it or not. If this is the case, doesn't it follow that I am free to stop making it? Suppose I own a small tool-and-die shop and feel harassed by union-organizing activities and more and more government regulation. I decide life is too short to stay in this business, so I decide to close up shop. Since it is my business, can't I argue that I am free to do what I want with it? This seems to be a persuasive prima facie case in favor of freedom to close or move.

But once one begins to reflect on this claim, we can also ask: Is such an action always ethically defensible, or are there limits?

First, it can be argued as we did in Chapter 3 that such an argument overlooks the fact that a business is not an independent entity, but an entity that involves relations. As we have said over and over, a relationship brings with it responsibility. For example, if two people *freely* choose to be friends, is it right for one to just walk out and terminate the relationship without a good reason or at least without some notification? The setting up of a relationship creates bonds and interdependencies, and to break these without a good reason is unethical. Thus, an owner cannot simply say I started it freely so I can quit it freely. Stopping a relationship is not as *free* an activity as starting one. I am *free* to marry whom I choose, but given the promises under which I freely entered into that relationship, there should be important reasons for overriding the promise and terminating the relationship. The existence of relationships, and the implied and expressed commitments necessary for relationships to exist, limit the freedom to terminate relationships. Thus, we argue, one is not simply free to terminate a relationship unless sufficient reasons exist for terminating it.

What are sufficient reasons? If the closing creates a great deal of harm, then the reasons for closing need to be more serious. Since society permits the owners of companies to make large profits from the use of citizens as employees and the use of the community, it can probably *morally* demand that the owner compensate in some way, say be persevering for a year or so.

There is also a danger of confusing the rights of large companies, where the stockholders are more like moneylenders than owners, with small companies where the owner is likely to be the manager with a link to his business that is not present in large corporations. It is not clear that the obligations of the small business entrepreneur are the same as the obligations of the large corporation. This relates to the issue of "capability," which we discussed in Chapter 2. For example, if a small factory owner defends a decision to close his business because he is suffering from "burnout" he is justified because he is not capable of going on any more. But in a large corporation that has replaceable managers such an argument is obviously irrelevant.

There is another objection to the freedom argument. It is the compensatory justice argument we alluded to above. The city or community contributes to the profit the business makes by allowing the use of its land and its citizens as employees. It is not entirely true that the benefits of employment and wages are compensation enough. The dependency of the community, which allows the business to develop, can be seen as a social cost, a debt that a company owes and comes due at plant-closing time.

Hence, the simple freedom argument—the right to close or move at will—by itself is insufficient to justify a plant closing. Considerations of harm and the requirements for compensation may override such a decision.

But can't a business make the profitability argument? For example, the Black and Decker argument was to reduce "excess production capacity," a move presumably that would maximize profits in the long run. Is not this argument appropriate? If a business doesn't make profits, it will not stay in business. That's true, but is a company justified in moving or closing, as in the case of Black and Decker, when it was making a profit, just for the sake of maximizing profits? How much profit is defensible? Is *maximizing* profit a sufficient reason for moving or shutting down? We would suggest that it is not a sufficient reason. There seems to be a stronger position to be considered in closing a plant. We will call it the *prevent harm* argument.

Even if a company argued that no compensation for past agreements was owed and no past promises of fidelity are being broken, there is still one argument against closing a plant. One might make an argument against moving or closing based on the responsibility to prevent harm that we discussed in Chapter 2. Using Simon, Powers, and Gunneman's principle, we could argue that a company, as well as any person, has a responsibility to prevent harm when four conditions are met: (1) proximity, (2) capability (3) need, and (4) last resort.

Suppose, now, we apply this principle to Black and Decker's situation. Suppose you are a manager or a member of Black and Decker's board of directors. You certainly have a fiduciary responsibility to the stockholders to make a profit. But does your company have any responsibility to the community of Allentown? Suppose we assume that G.E. gave back more than its fair compensation to

Allentown over the years, and the unforseen externalities were more than adequately provided for. Can one make a further argument that Black and Decker has an obligation to prevent harm to the employees of the plant as well as to the city?

That there is a *need* to keep industry in Allentown is obvious, particularly considering the closing of the Mack Truck plant. That Black and Decker is *proximate* is also obvious. But is the company *capable?* The fact that the Black and Decker small-appliance plant is making a profit, even if a small one, would indicate that keeping the plant open would not do serious damage to the company, other than slightly reducing its overall profit margins. Is keeping the plant open the *last resort?* That is an important question, and it seems it might be. But if Black and Decker wants to avoid being the last resort, then it might be seen as incumbent upon management to find other ways of preventing the harm—for example, seeking state aid, finding alternate buyers, or selling the plant to the employees. At any rate, while we might argue at length about the proper thing for Black and Decker to do, it seems clear that the managers and board of directors cannot simply assert that they are justified in closing the plant for no other reason than that they wish to do away with vertical operations, nor are they justified in simply closing or moving for the sake of maximizing profitability alone. Rather, what should be clear is that the obligation to the stockholders must be balanced against the obligation to the workers and the community. The fact that there was severance pay, even if that was negotiated by the union, underlies our contention that there are obligations that accrue to a community and its workers. Morality may demand more than law in this case, although recent legislation on plant closings also indicates that the responsibilities of corporations in plant closings are recognized more and more.

We certainly have not solved the Black and Decker plant-closing issue, but the case should show how a manager, CEO, or board member needs to address conflicts of obligation to stockholders and to the community.

Environmental Pollution

The philosopher Heraclitus in the fifth century B.C. pointed out that every creation of something new involves a destruction of the old. Consequently, every industrial production involves some pollution. Buckminster Fuller pointed out that pollution was just energy in the wrong place. Be that as it may, with the Industrial Revolution came the creation of huge amounts of industrial wastes that pollute the environment, a pollution that is both chemical and aesthetic. To the extent that there is no way to avoid pollution and its costs, we need to evaluate the benefits of the production to see if it is worth it. Our question becomes, How much pollution is justified in profit making? Since pollution is a harm, and production causes pollution, there are limits that need to be put on pollution caused by businesses.

It is important in the pollution issue to remember two things. The first is the old adage from the "Pogo" comic strip: "We have met the enemy and they are us." So one cannot put all the blame for pollution on the manufacturers and the managers. After all, if consumers, who are everybody, didn't purchase and use the products created there would be no pollution. We cause pollution as much as they.

Second, it is difficult to see how one could apply the *do no harm* principle. To the extent a desired product creates pollution, the harm is part of the bargain. We need to view pollution as we view the side effects of medication. Medication always has some side effects, but the issue is whether the benefits of the medication outweigh the costs of the side effects. So too with pollution. If the benefits do not outweigh the costs, the pollution seems unjustified. Ocean dumping, which was commonly accepted for years, is now becoming intolerable because of the harm it is doing to the environment.

For managers, perhaps the crucial problem of pollution is this: To what extent should the company take on pollution costs and who should pay the costs? This is a fairness issue. Because pollution is an externality, it has real costs involved in it. But who should pay them? For example, who should pay to clean up the damage done to Lake Erie by the steel plants, paper mills, etc.? Fairness would seem to demand that the user pay, since the cleanup is a real cost of the production. Thus, those who used the product—say the paper in our earlier example—should pay a higher price for the paper because pollution control and cleaning up past pollution make it more expensive. Ideally, the manager would compute the cost of reducing pollution and tack it on to the cost of the paper.

This suggestion has difficulties. First, some of the costs were not anticipated, and the pollution occurred years ago. Second, if a manager computed the cost of pollution control, while no one else in the industry did, the manager's firm would soon be out of business because competitors could create the same product much more cheaply. Thus, while we might say that ideally the cost of a product should reflect the costs of pollution reduction, that would seem impossible in some cases because it is too late and in other cases it would be impossible without government regulation.

While the ethical issues in pollution are fairly simple in the abstract, they are somewhat difficult to sort out in the concrete. Everyone is against pollution. But it is avoidable, if at all, only at a cost, and sometimes the cost is exorbitant. Where there are government regulations against pollution, it is fairly clear that the manager is obliged to obey them. Not to do so is clearly unethical. Thus, those who dumped pollution into the Allegheny River during the Ashland oil spill because they knew they would not be detected acted unethically. It was a classic example of putting one's self-interest ahead of moral considerations.

Still, to expect managers to do more than the law requires puts immense pressure on them. Their obligation to make a profit runs counter to their obligation not to harm, particularly in this situation where society allows the harm through lack of more stringent environmental regulations and/or enforcement. A classic dilemma arises—the obligation to make a profit versus the obligation not to harm. To the extent that a manager sacrifices *some* profit to minimize pollution, there is a clear justification. Here, more than in most cases, however, the manager is constrained by the free-rider problem. If as a society we want less pollution, we will have to strengthen our system of environmental regulation and enforcement.

OBLIGATIONS TO CONSUMERS

We turn now to investigate the various relationships that business and its managers have with their customers, remembering that we are all consumers. We begin with a general question: Does business have any responsibilities to its customers? On the one hand it seems obvious that it does; we expect businesses such as automobile companies to make safe cars and pharmaceutical companies to produce effective, uncontaminated drugs. In fact, we generally expect business to provide quality goods that are relatively safe and services that are reliable.

But it is not as simple as it all seems. What is the ethical ground of this expectation? Since a consumer is not coerced into purchasing a product and is free to buy or reject it, why couldn't someone argue that the responsibility for determining safety and reliability rests with the consumer rather than the producer? This is the classic view of caveat emptor—"let the buyer beware." It is a view that sees the consumer as free and not in need of paternalistic protection—that is, protection from someone presumably older and wiser such as a parent. Obviously there would be something wrong if we sold a dangerous motorbike to a five-year-old. Since five-year-olds are not mature and autonomous (self-directing) adults, we feel they are not capable of making free choices in these matters and they do need some protection. But don't we think that adults (the reasonable consumer) are capable of deciding for themselves?

The doctrine of *caveat emptor* has some plausibility in a world where the products of industry are simple enough to be examined directly for their safety and reliability and where there is sufficient time for consumers to do so. But even in that simple world, the doctrine of *caveat emptor* is morally flawed. *Caveat emptor* puts the *total* responsibility for determining safety and reliability on the consumer. Requirements of fairness would at least make safety and reliability a joint responsibility of the consumer and the producer.

However, the products of a highly technological and affluent society make such a joint responsibility an impossible idea. Consumers don't know and can't be expected to know enough about automobiles, computers, and over-the-counter medicines to take joint responsibility. In addition, modern consumers make hundreds of purchasing decisions every week. They can't be expected to research the safety and reliability of them all. For these reasons business must take more responsibility for safety and reliability, and the courts have so ruled.

In fact, the courts have moved from evaluating product liability on negligence grounds to applying a strict liability standard. *Strict liability* means that producers are responsible for even unintended and undetected product defects. Given the irresponsible behavior of many consumers—for example, using a power lawnmower as a hedge clipper—many people have argued that the strict liability rule places too heavy a burden on business. The debate as to the correctness of the court decisions is a fascinating one that raises issues of fairness in the assignment of responsibility when a consumer is harmed by a product. The movement of the court to the strict liability standard meets the approval of those philosophers who argue that in today's market it is appropriate to assign less responsibility to the consumer.

The plausibility of assigning more responsibility to manufacturers for quality and safety can be illustrated by considering some concrete cases.

Cordes Pacemakers

The Cordes Corporation on August 31, 1988, pleaded guilty to "concealing defects in thousands of heart pacemakers." This action is clearly wrong because it is fraudulent and it violates the expectation that consumers be informed about the potential harm in any product. The company "admitted to intentionally misleading both pacemaker buyers and the F.D.A. by *misrepresenting* the quality of the device."[9] Such an admission clearly recognizes that the managers acted unethically, and consequently recognizes the responsibility of managers to the consumers to deal with them forthrightly and honestly.

In the Cordes case it is clear that the managers failed in their obligation to deal honestly with their customers. But what are the obligations in the following cases—namely Pinto, Nestlé, and Tylenol?

The Pinto Gas Tank

In the 1970s the Ford Motor Company released its Pinto model that had a gas tank known to rupture easily and hence cause burn deaths. Ford, then under Lee Iacocca, wanted a compact auto to compete in the small-car market, one that weighed less than 2,000 pounds and cost (at the time) under $2,000.[10] The gas tank could have been made safer by putting it in a "bladder" or placing a shield between it and the rear bumper. Still, the car met federal regulations at the time (Ford lawyers did fight against stricter safety requirements). The company then conducted a cost-benefit analysis and determined that, whereas the necessary $11 improvement to make the gas tank safer would cost the company $137 million, the estimated 180 burn injuries and the estimated 180 burn deaths would cost only about $49 million. On the basis of those estimates, the Ford Motor Company decided against making the Pinto safer.

Whenever this example is presented to our students, it is generally agreed that the company acted unethically, and it is generally agreed that Ford had a responsibility to make its car safer. Indeed, there seems to be a general sentiment that products should be made as safe as possible. But it is important to reflect on what makes Ford's action unethical so that our hypothetical manager can understand the limits of one's obligations.

Obviously, if the improvement was not made, more profit was predicted by the cost-benefit study. (As a matter of fact, the cost estimates badly miscalculated the amounts of the court settlements and negative publicity; thus, in the end it cost Ford much more than the improvements would have cost. Still, it is interesting to note that the "scandal" did not drive Ford out of business, and the Pinto was one of the all-time, best-selling cars.)

If we review our ethical guidelines, there didn't seem to be coercion or fraud involved in Ford's behavior. The company's ads, although they didn't point out the dangers of the Pinto's gas tank, also didn't misrepresent the Pinto. However, it could be argued that since the gas tank danger was not easily discernible, there is a responsibility on the part of the company to meet customers' expectations of minimal safety, something most customers take for granted in buying mass-produced products, just as most customers take the purity or safety of medications for granted since they are unable to discern either the beneficial or harmful nature of them. Thus, one might claim that Ford owed its customers more forthrightness, or more concern about the safety of the product. Further, to reduce people's lives to cost factors seems heartless and immoral for the obvious reason that it reduces people to mere things where the worth of their lives is evaluated in monetary terms in order to maximize profits. After all, Ford was perfectly capable of preventing the harm without jeopardizing a satisfactory profit. Under the Simon, Powers, and Gunneman principle of the obligation to prevent harm, one could argue that Ford management acted unethically because it put profits above all other concerns. There was a need to prevent the harm of the burn accidents and deaths. Ford was the proximate cause and hence was proximately responsible. Ford also had the capability to prevent harm and was the last resort.

Of course, Ford might have argued that the decision about the gas tank was just one of many that had to be made and that if it had put safety first every time, the Pinto would have been prohibitively expensive and uncompetitive with other compact cars of its type. Ford could argue that the public will accept a lower margin of safety for a lower price. (There was an active market in Ford Pintos for some time after Ford stopped making them). However, at the very least, a corporation has an obligation to inform consumers of the trade-offs. This was not done in the Pinto case.

Nestlé Infant Care Formula

The Nestlé infant formula case raises an issue similar to the Ford case. It is an issue involving marketing in third-world countries. The marketing of breast-milk substitutes, namely infant formulas, to third-world nations was extremely successful in the 1960s and 1970s.[11] A rapidly expanding market was opening up. However, several problems arose when the formulas were used. The formula lacked the antibodies against local diseases found in mother's milk. In many of the countries water needed to mix the formula was not pure, and it was too expensive (fuel-wise) to sterilize all the implements. Finally, as the child grows, more infant formula is required. This leads either to more expensive costs before the infant is weaned or less nutritious formula caused by watering it down. As a result of these local conditions, thousands of babies became malnourished and many died.

Abbot Laboratories, a Nestlé competitor, developed its own code of marketing in underdeveloped countries, which was designed to avoid these bad effects. But Nestlé continued its mass-marketing techniques and a public outcry arose. On what grounds? It again seems that the public expects limits be put on the marketing and distribution of goods where the company can foresee harm occurring to consumers. In other words, the public demands that a limit be placed on profit making in order to avoid unnecessary harm.

Tampering with Tylenol

A discussion of the Tylenol case presents a very different corporate decision. When it was discovered that someone had tampered with bottles of Tylenol (by placing poison in Tylenol capsules) there was a total recall, refunding, and the development of a triple-seal safety cap, now a standard in the industry. Tad Tuleja points out that this recall was the result of the Johnson & Johnson credo (Tylenol's parent company), which states, "We believe our first responsibility is to the doctors, nurses and patients, to mothers and all others who use our products and services."[12] Johnson & Johnson recognizes that there is a responsibility to the consumers and users of a product. A pharmaceutical firm's very existence is tied to benefiting people.

Johnson & Johnson believes that in addition to its responsibility to produce a safe product, it has an additional duty to protect the product once it is on the market. In fact, after a second round of Tylenol tampering, Johnson & Johnson stopped making Tylenol capsules and made caplets, which are more tamper-proof. The contrast between Johnson & Johnson and Nestlé is instructive. Even if society should not expect every corporation to go as far as Johnson & Johnson, we can say that the manager is morally obliged not only to market a product without coercion or fraud, but is also obliged to produce one that is reasonably safe and reliable.

OBLIGATIONS TO EMPLOYEES

The final stakeholder relationship that places ethical requirements on modern business managers is the company's relationship to its employees. There is an anomaly here because managers, if they are not owners or investors, are themselves employees. But we will view the manager in this case as the loyal agent of the owners with the duty to represent the company's interests vis-á-vis the other employees.

As has been our usual procedure, we will look at this relationship and its structure to try to determine what are the rights of the respective parties in the relationship. Specific issues are familiar enough—employees claim they have rights to a fair wage, due process in hiring and firing, and respect of their privacy. If employees' have such rights, then managers are morally obliged to pay them just compensation for their work, must follow just procedures in hiring and firing, and should not interfere in employees' private lives or make demands on their private behavior.

But as we have seen frequently, to assert rights is neither to justify them nor to spell out their limits. Furthermore, the rights of employees frequently conflict with the rights of the employer. How is the manager to decide between the conflicting claims?

We begin by recognizing that any employer/employee relationship should be a contractual one, free of coercion and fraud, and consistent with the laws and general moral custom. However, unlike the manager's relationship to consumers and the community, the employer/employee relationship involves an authority/subordinate relationship. Hence, there is a greater possibility of the abuse of power and the usurpation of freedom by the use of coercion. For example, an unskilled employee who desperately needs a job is subject to many more subtle forms of coercion than is an employee who has a highly marketable skill. The former employee's freedom is much more in jeopardy. Because this is the case, it is wise to examine the conditions implicit in making a contract.

Contract makers must look upon each other as rights bearers. If we ask what human right is closely associated with contract making, the answer that comes back is the right to liberty. One cannot conclude a valid contract unless one is free to do so. That the market economy presupposes at least a negative right to liberty is accepted by almost the entire spectrum of political opinion from libertarians to welfare democrats.

Employees' Right to Liberty

Nevertheless, to move from the claim that every contract maker has a right to liberty to a list of specifications as to what the right to liberty entails is a difficult enterprise. In the most general formulation, the right to liberty is a right to noninterference. But obviously that right to noninterference is not open-ended. We are not free to do whatever we want. The classic specification of a right to liberty is provided by John Stuart Mill:

> The sole end for which mankind are warranted individually or collectively in interfering with the liberty of action of any of their number is self-protection. That the only purpose for which power can be rightfully exercised over any member of a civilized community, against his will, is to prevent harm to others. His own good, either physical or mental, is not a sufficient warrant.[13]

On this principle it would seem clear that aside from the exercise of power that the employee has agreed to—for example, agreeing to follow the boss's orders to perform a task—the employer has no right to interfere with the freedom of employees unless the exercise of that freedom does harm to the employer. Thus, if drug use does not harm the employer, it would seem that whether an employee uses drugs or not in his or her private life is none of the employer's business.

The concept of harm, though, provides a wide escape clause for the infringement on liberty. Corporations could and indeed have argued that apparent violations of individual liberty are necessary to prevent harm to the corporation. On the basis of that argument companies have regulated the dress, social life, family life, and political opinions of employees. Any employee action that adversely affects profit "harms" the corporation and could be restricted.

The problems are not just theoretical. Let us amplify this analysis with some practical questions raised by the senior vice-president of a major life insurance company when we discussed the issue of employee rights. Suppose that an employee of a major private health insurance company exercises his or her free speech to lobby actively for the passage of a government health insurance bill that would eliminate private health insurance companies. In effect, this employee seeks the elimination of his or her job and the jobs of colleagues. Does the insurance company or the employer have a right to constrain the employee's freedom of speech in this case?

Consider drug use. It is claimed that drug addiction costs American corporations billions of dollars in lost time, lowered performance, and hospitalization benefits. Because of these considerations does an employer have a right to conduct pre-employment drug testing? Can it perform random testing of existing employees?

Consider freedom of religious conscience. Suppose that a life insurance company acquires a health insurance company. This health insurance company pays medical bills for abortions. The claims processor from the parent company is a member of a church that holds abortion to be a deadly sin. On grounds of religious conscience, the processor refuses to put through claims for medical expenses to cover abortion. Does the company have an ethical right to fire this person, and if the company did, would it violate the employee's freedom of religious conscience?

What these examples show is that one must balance the harm done to a corporation's profits against the harm done to the employee when the corporation denies the employee the opportunity to exercise a particular liberty. Such balancing seems to be required to meet Mill's principle of liberty. This seems to mean that companies have only limited justification for interfering with employee's liberties whenever profits are adversely affected.

The Right To A Fair Wage

Once again, let us start from the laissez-faire point of view. In an ideal free market, people have their labor to sell, and its worth depends on the law of supply and demand. If it is unskilled labor and there are plenty of unskilled laborers around, the supply will far outstrip the demand and consequently its market value will be minimal. Laissez-faire proponents can argue that they will pay the going market price, and this is simply all that is demanded of them. If the laborers do not wish to work for that wage, they are free not to. Thus, the laissez-faire owner and managers can argue that they are perfectly ethical because they are playing by the rules of the system.

If those are the rules of the system, it is clear why Marxists object to it and why it needs reform. Such a rule is fundamentally immoral, because it turns a laborer into a commodity, into a mere means to an end, and thereby violates Kant's second imperative, "Act so as never to use another human being merely as a means to an end." When someone freely agrees to work for another, that person puts oneself in a delicate reciprocal relation of *mutual use.* That is, in going to work for someone you agree to let that person use you in return for certain reciprocal benefits. Now this is in line with Kant's imperative, for he adds the stipulation, "Not *merely* as a means." This means that as long as the person retains his or her personal autonomy and the reciprocity remains the mutual use, then the "you-scratch-my-back-and-I'll-scratch-yours" attitude prevails, and the relationship is fundamentally sound. But if the relative equality shifts and the one party becomes more and more dependent, the possibility of abuse looms large and a relationship freely entered into comes more and more to resemble a master/slave relationship where the one person "owns" the other.

If I need a job in order to live, I am not in a good position to bargain. Since my dependency can be exploited, I can be coerced and manipulated. This would allow management—to increase profit—by paying what the "market will bear." Such action in the past led to unionization and minimum wage laws.

Within our own society, unions were legitimized on the grounds of fairness as was the concept of the minimum wage. What exactly constitutes a fair minimum wage is an open question and one that would need debating beyond the limits of this work. Still it is instructive to note that the existence of a concept such as a "fair wage" indicates that there is general consensus in the belief that owners and/or managers must take into account more than considerations of profit and productivity in paying their employees. More recent views value more highly the employees' contributions in the creation of the profits and the capital base of companies. Such recognition led to the development of profit-sharing plans and other benefits. The underlying ethical point in this discussion has been that employees should not be seen as interchangeable with the other factors of production. Employees are human beings and are entitled to dignity and respect. They are not simply a means to profit.

The Right To Privacy

This brings us to our final consideration, the employee's right to privacy. Our discussion is placed in the context of a recent problem, namely whether it is ethical to subject employees to drug testing.

Returning to Mill's principle of liberty, we could argue that employees have a right to do whatever they wish as long as it does not harm the employer. Thus, many claim that if on one's own time an employee "does drugs," it is the employee's business; as long as it does not affect one's work, it is no business of the employer. Some defenders of the market point out that the really important aspect of the market is that it allows us to do business without being hampered by irrelevant considerations such as the beliefs, personal habits, politics, race, sex, or other behavioral and ideological idiosyncracies of the person we are doing business with. Thus, if a customer needs 200 electrical boxes, and you have them, the customer doesn't have to know what nationality you are or if you are a Democrat to make a deal for the electrical boxes. The only important questions are: Do you have the boxes? Are they legally yours to dispose of? How much are they?

If we apply this market model to the employer/employee relationship, the answer to the drug-testing issue becomes simple. If I have some work to sell to you, you purchase it. The only question is, Can I deliver? Thus, drug use only becomes "relevant" if it interferes with the delivery of the services you have contracted for. Hence, if I am purchasing a service and the quality of that service might be harmed if you are inhibited in your performance by drug use, it might be important for me to know that before I hire you. Other than the potential harm, though, the knowledge of drug use is not *job-relevant* and consequently prying into one's private life to determine it would not seem justified.

Nevertheless, there is a rejoinder to this. Throughout this chapter we have argued that the relationship between employer and employee is not a simple market relationship. It is not a one-shot meeting. It is a long-term relationship with a history, and thus to a certain extent it is not entirely possible to ignore all of one's beliefs and values and personal habits, particularly when the employee becomes an agent and representative of the employer. Thus, some knowledge of the private life and habits of the employee might be warranted. Still, to justify the infringement on privacy and liberty, the general requirement should be that the knowledge of the drug use is job-relevant and the use must be a potentially harmful use.

Having said all this, it is interesting to examine the policy of Drexelbrook Engineering Company, a 300-employee company in Horsham, Pa., which designs and manufactures electronic systems that measure and control levels of hazardous chemicals. Lewis Maltby, vice-president and general counsel of Drexelbrook, wrote an article entitled "Why Drug Testing Is a Bad Idea."

Maltby points out that a Drexelbrook employee who is "under the influence of drugs could cause a disaster as tragic as occurred in Bhopal [India]. But we won't do drug testing." Thus, although Maltby sees the validity of the avoid-harm principle and the justification of infringing on liberty if it can prevent harm, he still advises against it. Why? Because "When our top management considered the idea, we concluded that drug testing was not in the best interests of the company, would not make the products any safer and would actually hurt our performance and profits."[14]

We will simply summarize Maltby's objections. First, alcohol abuse is a more serious problem than controlled-substance abuse, "but no one proposes all employees be subjected to breathalyzer tests to keep their jobs." Second, drug testing suffers from accuracy problems. Third, the fundamental flaw is that it tests for the wrong thing. "A realistic program to detect workers whose condition puts the company or other people at risk would test for the condition that actually creates the danger....A serious program would recognize that the real problem is worker's impairment, and test for that."[15]

Maltby goes on to discuss the possibility that drug testing is bad management. It is an act of distrust on the part of management for it requires the vast majority of employees to prove their innocence when there's no reason to suspect they've done anything wrong. And finally, "It also violates their rights by reaching out from the employer's legitimate sphere of control at the workplace and telling employees what they can and can't do on their own time in their own homes."[16]

What program does Drexelbrook practice? Let us quote Maltby rather extensively, for he sets up what seems to be a responsible attitude toward the rights of employees

> We practice good management. We always say that people are our most important asset, and at Drexelbrook, we try to put that idea into practice.
>   We begin by trying to create a positive atmosphere. We want every employee to give us 100% every day. And we want each of them to make every decision with the best interests of the company at heart. By and large, we get that. But that kind of commitment doesn't come easily. We have to earn it.

One way we earn it is by treating our employees as adults. We trust them to do their jobs right and don't subject them to a lot of unnecessary rules. We trust our employees to know what working hours and style of dress are required for them to get their jobs done. Another way to earn that commitment is by respecting their rights. We scrupulously avoid prying into our employees' private lives. Finally, we care about them....

This approach to employee relations is not philanthropy—it's good business. Our employees routinely go above and beyond the call of duty to help our customers....

Our experience is confirmed by a recent American Management Association survey of 1,000 companies that found the most effective program to fight workplace drug abuse combines employee education with trained supervisors who know how to identify and constructively confront employees who fail to meet performance standards.

The fact is, most companies don't do drug testing. And, according to the American Management Association study, a third of those who do think there is no value in it.[17]

The evolving consensus about employee rights seems to be away from laissez-faire acceptance of an employer's unlimited right to treat an employee as the employer wishes, and to put some limits on that employer. But what are the limits? Each case seems to call for different considerations. But if we return to Friedman's proviso, which demands that businesses operate within the law and ethical customs, we can argue that business activity should conform to the laws and basic moral norms of society. Once this background condition is understood, a business cannot restrict the freedom of an employee when that restriction requires the employee to perform some act that violates either the law or a basic moral norm of society. An employee cannot be ordered to falsify experimental data relating to product safety or to discriminate against a fellow employee on the basis of race. The fact that the falsification of the data or the discrimination would improve profits is irrelevant.

But what about restrictions on individual liberty that do not violate fundamental norms or legal statutes? Some further specification of the extent of a person's right to liberty is provided by the U.S. Constitution. Since business activity takes place within American society, presumably business activity should be conducted consistent with the Bill of Rights, which specifies our right to liberty. For example, the rights of free speech and religious expression are specific examples of the rights to liberty that are embodied in the Constitution. As such, these rights should be honored by business practice.

The recognition of these constitutional rights by business would result in major changes in business practice, at least in many firms. The insurance company employee's right to lobby for an insurance bill that would eliminate private companies is more fundamental than is the insurance company's desire not to have the issue discussed. Indeed, in this case we would argue that the insurance company has no rights claims that are relevant in this case. The employee is not interfering with the company's right to do business, and the company has a right of free speech equal to that of the employee to bring its case before the American public. Outside the workplace, the employee's constitutionally guaranteed rights ought to have an even greater priority to override any right of an employer to prevent employee conduct that might reflect adversely on the employer's business.

Even within the workplace, constitutionally protected rights should be given a more prominent place. Surely the employee who objects to processing abortion claims can be accommodated. Someone else can do the abortion claims, and the objecting employee can be given other responsibilities. Indeed, greater flexibility in scheduling and job description could protect employee rights, reduce role conflicts for working mothers, and perhaps even increase morale, productivity, and profit.

But what about those difficult cases in which the rights of employees clash with the rights of management? After all, the employer is a party to the contract between employer and employee, and the contract argument works just as well in establishing employer rights as it does in establishing employee rights. In other words, society does give a business a right to pursue profit as well as give individuals a right to free action. The interesting and difficult practical situations occur when rights come into conflict.

It seems to us that the wrong way to decide such conflicts is for the boss to give an order or issue an edict. Rather, some mechanism should be available for airing the dispute in a way that the rights claims of both employee and management can be heard. Grievance procedures in all their variety are hardly a novelty on the corporate scene. We have no formula for an ideal grievance procedure beyond demands of fairness and due process, but employees have a moral right to help decide the rules that govern their conduct.

CONCLUSION

In this chapter we have not attempted to resolve specific moral issues. Rather, we have argued that the manager is bound by moral considerations, considerations of justice, fairness, and avoiding harm in dealing with separate stakeholders. We have shown that there seems to be a developing awareness of these responsibilities.

Nevertheless, most companies still aren't as enlightened as is Drexelbrook, and the basic drives for profit and "bottom line" concerns remain powerful motivators. Thus, a question arises. Even if the manager sees something as morally desirable, like paying employees more or not polluting, what would move the manager to do that if it didn't enhance profits? What, in short, will help companies and managers to do the moral thing? We turn to that issue in the next chapter.

NOTES

[1]Milton Friedman, "The Social Responsibility of Business Is to Increase Its Profits," *New York Times Magazine,* September 13, 1970, p. 33.

[2]Restatement (Second) of Agency (1958) 395.

[3]Friedman, "Social Responsibility," 33.

[4]James M. Roche, "The Competitive System, to Work, to Preserve, and to Protect," *Vital Speeches of the Day* (May 1971): 445.

[5]For example, see Ronald Duska, "Whistleblowing and Employee Loyalty" in *Ethical Theory and Business,* 3rd ed., Tom L. Beauchamp and Norman E. Bowie, eds. (Englewood Cliffs, N.J.: Prentice Hall, 1988), 299–303.

[6]Norman E. Bowie, *Business Ethics,* 1st ed. (Englewood Cliffs, N.J.: Prentice Hall, 1982), 142.

[7]This quotation is from a discussion draft prepared for the Hastings Center Project on "The Teaching of Ethics," by Charles W. Powers and David Vogel, p. 40. This comment was omitted from the published version.

[8]This account is based on reports in the *Philadelphia Inquirer* of January 29 and March 26, 1985.

[9]*Philadelphia Inquirer,* September 1, 1988, p. 3.

[10]Mark Dowie, "Pinto Madness," *Mother Jones,* September/October 1977, p. 49.

[11]For a presentation of this case, see Gerald Cavanagh and Arthur F. McGovern, *Ethical Dilemmas in the Modern Corporation* (Englewood Cliffs, N.J.: Prentice-Hall, 1988), 99.

[12]Tad Tuleja, *Beyond the Bottom Line* (New York: Facts on File Publications, 1985), 79.

[13]John Stuart Mill, *On Liberty,* ed. Currin V. Skield (Indianapolis: Bobbs Merrill Library of Liberal Arts, 1956), 13.

[14]Lewis Maltby, "Why Drug Testing Is a Bad Idea," *Inc.,* June 1987, p. 152.

[15]Ibid., 153.

[16]Ibid., 153.

[17]Ibid., 153.

Chapter Five

From Theory
To Practice

Thus far we have looked at what a corporation is, what its purpose is, how it relates to the rest of society, what general moral principles govern its operations, and how those principles affect the manager's responsibilities to the various stakeholders in the business. We would like to address briefly in this final chapter the question of how to get these moral considerations put into practice.

Let's return to that old cliche, "There's no such thing as business ethics." We are by now aware that that can't be true if what we mean by it is that corporations and their managers and employees have no moral responsibilities. But there is another possible meaning to the phrase. All too often people mean to say that ethical behavior isn't practiced in business—that is, there may be ethical rules that should be followed, but given the way things are done in the "real" world, most business people don't act ethically. Most people in business are driven by one and only one concern, and that's the bottom line—making a profit—and that concern overrides any ethical concerns.

We think such a belief is not only overly cynical but empirically false. The experience we have had with large numbers of business people is that they are fundamentally honest, fair, reliable, keep their promises, and set fairly high ethical standards for themselves and others. For example, most accountants, to mention only one group of business professionals, are highly scrupulous in their business operations.

Still, a small number of unscrupulous business persons have no concern for ethically correct behavior. They are only interested in making a buck by freeloading off the good reputation of others in the business community, using inside information, conning trusting clients, fudging reports to ingratiate themselves to bosses, inflating expense accounts, falsifying information to float loans, or some such behavior. But it is difficult to think of anyone in a responsible position who condones that type of behavior. When those in positions of responsibility sigh and become somewhat cynical about the number of their colleagues who operate unethically, what they are usually expressing is a frustration at having to compete with such unethical competitors. It would be naive to think that we will ever be rid of all such unscrupulous business people. Greed is, after all, a part of the human condition.

Rather than considering the behavior of these unscrupulous business types, we will concentrate on the plight of the ordinary business person. There are probably times in every business person's life when unethical behavior would be the line of least resistance. Moreover, there are probably times when the well-meaning business person will succumb to such temptations. It is folly to expect all people to fulfill their obligations all the time. Human beings are not perfect. They have what Aristotle called "weakness of will."

Nevertheless, in a case of someone following self-interest rather than fulfilling obligations, the proper response is to judge the behavior as "wrong" or "selfish," exact repentance or punishment, and expect better behavior in the future, rather than concede that "everybody does it."

One must be cautious in business because the market system rests on the pursuit and legitimation of self-interest. However, when that pursuit of self-interest turns to unfettered greed the problems we saw in Chapter 3 follow. What we will show in this chapter is that a single individual or a single firm alone will find it next to impossible, unless they are heroic, to overcome or counteract the generally accepted practices of business, even where those are unethical. Thus, business needs to police itself or be policed, so that limitations on self-interested profit are carried out where appropriate.

There are three ways of being motivated to do the right thing. The first is a strong will; the second, fear of punishment; and the third, peer pressure to abide by the demands of the society. For business, government regulation provides the threat of punishment, and self-regulation by the business community provides the peer pressure. We will investigate these two means of providing motives for business to be moral. But before doing that let us show why we would be naive to expect simple will power on the part of an executive to be a sufficient motivator of the right action.

Take the following example, which is partly based on fact. Forty years ago there was a paper mill located on the shores of one of the Great Lakes. That paper mill would dump its sludge into the lake, for that was the cheapest way of getting rid of its wastes. But everyone living around the lake, those who used the lake for fishing or swimming, could see that the sludge was polluting the lake. It turned the blue water a foam-covered dingy brown, and the radius of the brown circle that formed at the base of the pipe spewing forth the sludge grew by hundreds of yards each year, enveloping and polluting more and more of the lake.

The president of the paper mill was a devoted citizen of the community and the father of several children who, because they lived on the mill grounds, could not swim or fish in the lake. Neither could they enjoy the aesthetic delight of looking out from their house and seeing clear blue lake waters. The president *had* to know that the dumping was harming the lake. As a citizen and father, he was probably concerned with the bad effects of this pollution. Yet, at that time, as a businessman what could he do? There was no industrywide regulation against dumping sludge. There were no government regulations against dumping. If he decided unilaterally to cease the dumping and find a safer, cleaner, and more aesthetically pleasing mode of waste disposal, the price of his paper would rise and make his product uncompetitive. He might have been morally heroic, but he would also have gone out of business. He had responsibilities to his stockholders that required that he ignore the pollution for the sake of profit.

This example should make it clear that in certain circumstances one cannot expect will power to be the only motivating force nor expect individuals to sacrifice their very livelihoods for morality, nor should we expect individual businesses to sacrifice their survival for morality if there are no industrywide rules or governmental regulations.

Given the expectation of weakness of will, how can society be assured that businesses and business people will behave as they ought to behave?

What can society reasonably expect concerning the moral behavior of the individual business person? As we just saw, society can not expect a high level of moral behavior on the part of the individual business person if the practices and reward structures of business firms do not support that behavior. In other words, individual ethical behavior will be impaired if such behavior either hinders or does not advance an individual's business interests. Further, a particular firm's behavior will be impaired if such behavior hinders or does not advance that firm's financial position. Hence, the discussion in this chapter is directed toward possible structural changes that entire industries as well as individual firms have made or could make to enhance the probability of ethical behavior on the part of both the firms and the individuals within those firms.

SELF-REGULATION AND CODES OF ETHICS

One of the most popular ways of developing industrywide ethical principles is by developing codes of ethics, sets of rules that members of a specific industry or profession are to follow. Almost any discussion of morality eventually focuses on the desirability of basing morality on rules. We will try to show that business codes of ethics can be useful devices to assist individuals to behave ethically in the business setting. This is not to say that rules alone are sufficient as devices to aid the individual in the practice of moral behavior, nor that business codes of ethics are sufficient for that purpose in the business setting, but they do have some advantages.

The first advantage of a code is that it can motivate through using peer pressure. A code holds up a generally recognized set of behavioral expectations that must be at least minimally considered in decision making. For example, one could not easily defend one's practices as an accountant if that person regularly violated the "Standards of Ethical Conduct for Management Accountants."

A second advantage to codes is that they provide more stable permanent guides to right or wrong than do human personalities or continual ad hoc decisions. If we take the notion of weakness of will seriously it should be apparent that people are not completely objective. People tend to take the short-run point of view. The passions of a situation get in the way of a wise decision. These frailties of human nature require that decisions about ethics generally be a matter of law or rules.

Third, codes of ethics really do provide guidance, especially in ethically ambiguous situations. By tying a code of ethics to a job description, what counts as appropriate ethical conduct is clarified. Along these lines, empirical research supports the view that a clear set of rules does make a difference as to whether or not an employee will engage in an ethically dubious action. For example, W. Harvey Hegarty and Henry P. Sims, Jr., have done research with graduate students confronted with decision-making opportunities. His results show that a clear company policy forbidding kickbacks lowers the tendency of the graduate students to permit kickbacks.[1]

Fourth, codes of ethics not only guide the behavior of employees but they also control the autocratic power of employers. In theory at least, a business code of ethics can provide an independent ground of appeal when one is urged by an employer or supervisor to commit an unethical act. "I'm sorry, but company policy strictly forbids it" is a gracious way of ending a conversation about a "shady" deal.

A fifth advantage of codes of business ethics is that they could help specify the social responsibilities of business itself. One of the problems in business ethics is that no one seems to know what the rules are. As we have seen, most business leaders recognize that the social responsibilities of business must expand and that business executives should be held to higher ethical standards than in the past. However, a blanket ethical demand that business solves all social problems is arbitrary and unrealistic. Hence, business codes of ethics acceptable both to the business community and to the general public would help define what corporate social responsibility involves and bring some order out of the chaos.

Sixth, and perhaps most important, the development of business codes of ethics is clearly in the interest of business itself. There is virtual unanimity in the business community that unethical business practices threaten to bring about increased government regulation of business. For reasons we will discuss later, government regulation of business ethics is not viewed as the most desirable form of regulation. When compared with the specter of government regulation, many business people agree that codes of ethics at least deserve a second look.

Codes of good business practice that have these advantages are not new. After all, one of the purposes of the Better Business Bureau is to protect both the consumer and the legitimate business operator from the fly-by-night operator. A lesson we can learn from the Better Business Bureau is that business ethics is not only in the interest of the consumer but can also be in the vital interest of the business community. As we saw, business activity depends on a high level of trust and confidence. If a firm or entire industry loses the confidence of the public, it will have a difficult time in selling its products.

In many cases, an industrywide code of ethics will provide the appropriate device for maintaining public trust. Such codes, when enforced properly, provide a means for assuring that all who subscribe to the code will behave in the morally appropriate way. In that way the firms would remain competitive with one another and would reap the benefits of morality as well.

Despite the acknowledged advantages of codes of business ethics, these codes are often treated with great skepticism by many business people and by representatives of the consuming public as well. What are their objections?

Initially, there is a very serious practical objection to industrywide codes of ethics. Business leaders are reluctant to sit down together to write such codes for fear that they will be in violation of antitrust laws. However, we understand that antitrust laws allow discussion and development of industrywide codes of ethics under government supervision. Since it seems highly likely that some way can and should be found to permit the development of industrywide codes without violating antitrust laws, the objection is not too troubling.

A second criticism of professional codes of ethics is that they are too broad and amorphous. Consider four of the seventeen standards of the Public Relations Society of America (PRSA).

1. A member has a general duty of fair dealing toward his or her clients or employees, past and present, his or her fellow members, and the general public.
2. A member shall conduct his or her professional life in accord with the public welfare.
3. A member has the affirmative duty of adhering to generally accepted standards of accuracy, truth, and good taste.
4. A member shall not engage in any practice that tends to corrupt the integrity of channels of public communication.[2]

Because it uses terms such as "fair dealing," "public welfare," "generally accepted standards," and "corrupt the integrity," the code of standards of the PRSA is charged with being too broad and hazy.

Two points can be made here. First, even if the PRSA code is guilty as charged, that does not mean that all codes are similarly guilty. Second, and more important, language is always general and in need of interpretation. Moreover, whenever we have a definition, there are certain borderline cases. When is a person bald or middle aged? We used to think that 35 was middle aged. Now we are not so sure. The point of these comments is to show that some of the criticisms of business codes are usually not criticisms of the code but of the language itself. This generality of the criticism provides the clue for mitigating the problem. After all, the institution known as the law is a well-entrenched social institution, and it is an institution that is grounded heavily in language. So, after all, is business practice. Contracts, collective-bargaining agreements, warranties, and the like are all linguistic devices that facilitate the practice of business. If language usage is as broad and amorphous as the critics contend, what accounts for the operational success of law and business?

We submit that the answer to this question is twofold. First, language is not so broad and amorphous after all. The terms of a language have what H.L.A. Hart refers to as a "settled core of meaning."[3] Consider the rule that forbids vehicles from entering a public park. Clearly there are some borderline cases—roller skates, a baby carriage. But there are clear cases as well. Automobiles are forbidden. If one accepts the notion of a "settled core of meaning," then most uses of words are clear enough. It is only at the borderline where controversies concerning application develop. The message for those constructing codes of business ethics seems quite clear. If the code is constructed with the settled core of meaning of the words in mind, ambiguity will be cut to a minimum. If the code of ethics is taken seriously, the choice of words will be taken seriously as well.

Still, ambiguities will remain. Codes will still need interpretation, and hence procedures must be adopted for interpreting what the code means and what the code requires. However, this is no more of a problem for a code of business ethics than it is for other uses of language. The law itself, even at the highest level represented by the Constitution, requires a Supreme Court to make a final decisive interpretation. Although frequently the law is the social institution most often appealed to when disagreements concerning the terms of a contract arise, other possibilities arise. The Better Business Bureau has an appeal procedure that can culminate in binding arbitration, a provision used frequently.

The third and perhaps most serious criticism of business codes of ethics is that they cannot be adequately *enforced*. A code of ethics without adequate enforcement is hardly a code at all. An effective code of ethics must be enforced and must have real penalties attached to it in order for it to bring about conformity.

But can this be accomplished? We have two problems. There is, first, the problem of industries enforcing the proper behavior on individual firms that have a tendency to ride free, and second is the problem of a company enforcing its codes on its employees.

The second problem is obviously simpler. We turn to that immediately. For a firm to simply have a code with penalties on the books is not enough. In a home where discipline is taken seriously, a certain atmosphere pervades. We submit that in a company where ethics is taken seriously, a certain atmosphere will also pervade. We cannot identify all the signs that indicate that the right atmosphere exists, but we can mention some possibilities discussed in the literature.

First, businesses that have as their guide "if it's not illegal, it's not unethical" will not have a proper atmosphere. Such an attitude is not appropriate because at most the law prescribes minimum standards of ethical behavior. Many of the serious problems in business ethics lie outside the law. For example, we have previously seen that in the Ford Pinto case the company limited its concern solely to cost factors within the limits of the law, thus missing the central moral concerns involved in the case. Also consider the issue of employee rights. Here the law provides no such extensive rights. However, morality requires that in the practice of business such rights be taken seriously. Thus, a business that limits its ethics to legality has an extremely limited view of ethics.

Moreover, the attitude "if it's not illegal, it's ethical" is ultimately self-defeating. By depending only upon the law, one actually encourages the growth of government regulations to which most business people strongly object. The American Institute of Certified Public Accountants recognized this when it described its code of professional ethics as a voluntary assumption of self-discipline above and beyond the requirements of law.

Another sign that the right atmosphere exists would be how seriously the management of the company, beginning with the CEO, takes ethical behavior and the codes. If the code is just window dressing, there for the sake of public respectability, and the senior executives wink at it, that attitude will filter down and the force of the code will slowly evaporate.

Thus, we would expect some demonstration on the part of management that the code will be enforced effectively. Employees are perfectly aware of productivity goals, and an employee who misses the goal is penalized. Because it is a fact about much business practice that there is little penalty for bad ethical decisions but often severe penalties for failure to meet sales or profit goals, there is a built-in pressure for unethical behavior. Low-level managers and supervisors recognize the consequences for behavior expressed in the following syllogism.

1. If a code of ethics is really to be taken seriously, management must give it the same status as directives that affect profits.
2. Management does not give codes of ethics the same status as directives that affect profits.
3. Therefore, management is not really serious about its codes of ethics.

By now it should be clear that if codes of ethics are to work, they must be enforced. Exhortations are not enough. But how is enforcement to be carried out? Perhaps someone in the corporation should be responsible for ensuring that all employees of the company subscribe to high ethical standards. Many suggestions for institutionalizing this concern with ethics have been mentioned, and some have been implemented. It is not our task in this book to evaluate such suggestions. But we will give a short list of some of them.

Theodore Purcell has advocated electing an "angel's advocate" to the board of directors.[4] This person would be an adviser in matters of business ethics, whose responsibility would be to make sure that the ethical perspective be brought to bear on all major corporate decisions.

Purcell's idea has been adopted by some companies. Perhaps the best-known "angel's advocate" is Leon Sullivan, pastor of the Zion Baptist Church in Philadelphia and the first black director of the General Motors Corporation. However, despite Sullivan's endorsement based on experience, the number of companies placing public-interest members on their boards has not grown significantly in the past few years.

An important objection to public-interest directors is that by institutionalizing matters of ethics in one person, the rest of the company employees are "off the hook." A public-interest director becomes the ethics person and everyone else can direct his or her attention to the more important work of increasing profits. If such an attitude should in fact develop, the very purpose of having a public-interest director would be thwarted. Instead of increasing the awareness of ethical issues, the public-interest director would actually decrease such awareness. If factual evidence indicated that this criticism was correct, at the very least the public-interest director would need additional institutional support. Otherwise, this attempt at self-regulation would not be effective.

A second suggestion, advanced by Christopher Stone, for institutionalizing the concern for enforcing codes is to legally require a company to establish structures so that certain moral judgments do in fact get made. Stone cites some examples of what controls he has in mind:

1. Current regulations of the Food and Drug Administration that require the establishment of quality control units whose powers and responsibilities are set by government authorities;
2. Criteria that set qualifications as to who may and who may not hold certain corporate positions;
3. Federal Communications Commission regulations that insist that someone in authority know the lyrics of the records played on the air;
4. National Institute of Mental Health guidelines for genetic research.

Stone maintains that his approach represents an innovation that will raise the level of corporate conduct.

> All these forms of control can be classified as what I call "organizational adjustment measures." Unlike the traditional approaches, their focus is not so much on what organizations do, but on the ways organizations decide.[5]

In summary, what we see in this discussion of enforcement is that codes of ethics by themselves are not sufficient devices to provide the climate for a desirable record on business ethics. Codes of ethics must be buttressed by internal mechanisms within the corporation if they are to be effective. They must be (1) interpreted adequately and (2) enforced effectively by ethical persons. Ethical behavior is not simply a matter of good laws. Nor is ethics simply a matter of having good people. If the ethical perspective is to be effective in human behavior, both good laws and good people are necessary.

This discussion should represent the answer to a common criticism of codes of business ethics—namely that they are mere window dressing or public-relations gimmicks, if you will. Of course, many are just that. But the philosophical question is whether or not there is something in the logic of codes of ethics that requires them to be nothing more than public-relations gimmicks. We submit that codes need not be doomed to public-relations stunts. Codes governing employees within a company seem to have a chance of success. If these codes are well written, have an official body for interpretation and application, and are adequately enforced, they do represent an effective means for obtaining ethical behavior.

A more difficult problem arises with the enforcement of codes that apply industrywide. The purpose of an industrywide code is to enforce a standard of behavior in order that no one be penalized in the marketplace for ethical behavior. If a code addresses a problem that is common to all firms in the industry, all companies must agree to it if it is to be effective. Otherwise the companies that don't agree will have a competitive advantage. How do we force all the companies in the industry to adopt the code?

And suppose all firms did adopt it. There would have to be a policing mechanism so that companies breaking the code could be caught and punished. Some representative body of the industry would need to have enforcement powers, including the power to inflict punishment on code breakers. However, getting unanimous agreement on a code with punishments for violators and electing a representative body to enforce it is extraordinarily difficult.

GOVERNMENT REGULATION

To the extent that business is unable to regulate itself, the most obvious alternative to the self-regulation of business is government regulation. Government regulation is both widely used and widely criticized. In this section we consider some of the advantages, disadvantages, and limitations of government regulation as a means for ensuring acceptable ethical behavior on the part of business.

Before discussing government regulation per se, it is worth pointing out that business practice presupposes an effective government. As we have seen, business activity would not take place in a society where certain moral practices were not operative since business activity requires a minimally just society. It is one of the tasks of government to enforce this moral minimum—to provide for law and order. We should also recognize that business is a rule-governed activity. When disputes arise in business about what the rules require—for example, what is or is not entailed by a given contract—it is the function of government to serve as an umpire for interpreting the rules. The judiciary is the branch of government where business people who disagree about the terms of a contract can get their disputes resolved. It is also that branch of government to which a business person can turn to get a contract enforced against an unwilling contractee. Except for anarchists, even persons holding the most conservative positions on the scope of government authority agree that capitalism requires a government with sufficient authority and power to maintain a minimum sense of justice, to enforce business contracts, and to serve as an umpire to interpret the rules of the business game.

Perhaps the most important role of the government is to preserve competition and its benefits. In its initial phase, government regulation was designed to protect both business and the public from anti-competitive practices. This protection included the regulation of natural monopolies (for example, the utilities) where it makes no sense to have competing companies but it is important to protect the customer from unfair prices. Later this anti-monopolistic regulatory task was expanded to protect the public from unfair competitive practices as well.

Government regulation expanded to focus on fraud, deception, and dishonesty. In this latter sphere, the public is perhaps most familiar with the government ban on deceptive advertising regulated by the Federal Trade Commission (FTC).

It is important to emphasize that this type of government regulation—when conducted fairly and efficiently—both ought to be and in fact is supported by the business community. Such government regulation ought to be supported by the business community because it is regulation designed to support the rules of business activity itself. Practices that undermine competition either through monopoly or deceit cut away at a central tenet of business practice. From a market perspective, failure to support attempts to control and thwart such anti-competitive practices would be self-defeating.

Theory, in this regard, is supported by practice. Complaints regarding deceptive advertising often are brought to the attention of government regulators by the competitors of the alleged offender. It was competing oil companies that successfully challenged Chevron's STP advertising claims. Similarly, it was competing drug companies that complained to the FTC about the claims of Sterling Drug on behalf of Bayer aspirin. Sterling used a report in the *New England Journal of Medicine,* which received partial financial support from the FTC itself, as "objective" proof for the superiority of Bayer aspirin. Competing drug companies alleged that the ads were misleading and deceptive. That dispute went all the way to the Supreme Court, which turned down the complaints of the competing drug companies (*F.T.C.* v. *Sterling Drug*). It was also Holly Farms that brought complaints against Perdue's ads, which intimated that because Perdue's chickens were yellower (actually the result of simply adding xanthophyll to its chicken feed) they were healthier. This untrue implication was challenged as being unfair. The Bayer aspirin dispute and the Holly Farms complaint provide perfect illustrations of business reliance on government regulation and of its use of the judiciary to settle a dispute on a rule of business practice. Such government regulation is clearly in the interest of business.

Government regulation can also serve another interest of business. In our discussion of the paper mill and pollution, we saw how a business could be in a dilemma with respect to some socially desirable act it wished to undertake. For example, if government sets universal air-quality-control standards, all firms polluting the air would be required to install scrubbers. In this way, government regulation enables some companies to do the good they wanted to do but could not do because the competitive penalties would be too high.

Another advantage of government regulation is that it forces indifferent or maleficent corporations to adhere to the minimum requirements of corporate social responsibility. Much of the growth of government regulation can be attributed to the fact that society has broadened its notion of corporate social responsibility, and hence it has increased its demand for government protection.

In summary, the expansion of government regulation is the result of at least three factors. First, it results from the universally recognized authority of government to interpret and enforce the rules of business activity, especially rules to preserve competition. Second, it results from requests from socially enlightened corporations that need government-imposed standards to enable them to take socially desirable actions without incurring serious competitive disadvantages. Third, it results from the demands of the general public that it be protected against a growing list of what are viewed as undesirable corporate practices.

To paraphrase Thomas C. Schelling's case for government regulation: You need government regulation when the firm may lack the discipline, the information, the incentives, or the moral authority to command performance or restraint on the part of everyone whose cooperation is needed.[6]

Despite the advantages for business of some forms of government regulation, regulation is generally looked upon unfavorably. Let us summarize some of the more common objections. The sheer volume of regulatory legislation is impossible to keep up with. The costs of regulation are significant and growing. The regulatory commissions are not accountable to anyone. There is a convergence of regulator and regulated interest. Independent regulatory commissions misallocate resources. There are nonsense regulations, conflicts among regulations, and last but not least, since power corrupts, the inevitable bureaucratic imperialism. All of this tends to lead to a disrespect for the law.

While some of these arguments are well taken, none of them indicate that all regulation is unjustified. What we need are criteria that enable us to distinguish good regulations from bad regulations. Because regulations are in fact laws, if we can set up criteria for good laws, we can use these as tests for evaluating and reforming both regulations and regulators.

Criteria for Good Law

In a penetrating analysis of law (*The Morality of Law*), Lon Fuller identified eight formal conditions that any legal system must fulfill if it is to be considered a good legal system.[7] These eight conditions include (1) laws must be general (laws are not made to apply to one individual), (2) laws must be publicized, (3) laws cannot be made retroactively, (4) laws must be understandable, (5) the set of laws should not contain rules that are contradictory, (6) laws must be within the power of citizens to obey them, (7) laws must maintain a certain stability through time, and (8) laws as announced must be in agreement with their actual administration.

Fuller's eight formal conditions for a good legal system have such a ring of self-evidence about them that explanatory comments can be kept to a minimum. However, in the course of supplying some explanatory comment, the extent to which government regulation violates these eight conditions for good law will become obvious. The condition of generality is clearly related to the analyses of justice and the "universality" required by Kant's categorical imperative discussed in Chapter 3. Rules are not directed toward a single person but rather are to apply to a class of persons. Relevantly similar persons are to be treated similarly. What is a reason in one case must be a reason in all similar cases.

Despite this requirement of generality, much regulatory law proceeds in an opposite direction. Fuller notes,

> In recent history perhaps the most notable failure to achieve general rules has been that of certain of our regulatory agencies, particularly those charged with allocative functions....[T]hey were embarked on their careers in the belief that by proceeding at first case by case they would gradually gain an insight which would enable them to develop general standards of decision. In some cases this hope has been almost completely disappointed; this is notably so in the case of the Civil Aeronautics Board and the Federal Communications Commission.[8]

If general rules are essential to good regulatory law as has been argued, then the case-by-case method is inadequate. If the government takes a position regarding water pollution from one of Bethlehem Steel's plants, the president of Bethlehem Steel should be able to conclude that the government will take a similar position when the same situation exists at other competing steel plants. If Fuller's description is right and if the state of regulatory law is such that the president of Bethlehem Steel could *not* conclude that a similar position would be taken, the regulatory law is seriously deficient.

The second condition is that laws be publicized. One cannot obey the law if one does not know what the law is. Regulatory law does conform—on the whole—to this condition. The regulations do appear in federal documents such as the *Federal Register.* However, any academic researcher who has worked with government documents knows that finding a rule or regulation is often no easy task. Large corporations have legal teams to assist them in knowing what the law is. However, as government regulations grow, small business firms suffer a distinct handicap in their capability for knowing the law. To the extent the regulations change rapidly over time, the publicity requirement becomes harder and harder to meet.

Third, laws should not be made retroactively, and generally they are not. The reason for this requirement is clear. Laws are designed to guide behavior. A retroactive law violates the fundamental purpose of laws, for it obviously cannot guide conduct. It punishes behavior that was legal at the time it was done. Business leaders complain that government regulators at least approach violating this condition when they threaten firms with penalties for environmental damage when there was no way for the firm to have known that some of its activities were causing environmental damage. A company should not be penalized for damage it caused to the earth's ozone layer when it produced fluorocarbons in the 1960s.

The fourth requirement that laws be understandable is, to many business executives, the condition that government regulations most often violate. Loaded with jargon and bad grammar, these regulations often present a nightmare for highly trained corporate legal staffs and an impossible situation for small companies. A sample selection will serve to illustrate the point:

911.341 Lime Regulation 39.

(a) During the period May 1, 1979, through June 17, 1979, no handler shall handle:

(1) Any limes of the group known as true "seeded" limes (also known as Mexican, West Indian, and Key limes and by other synonyms), grown in the production area, which do not meet the requirements of at least U.S. No. 2 Grade for Persian (Tahiti) Limes, except as to color: Provided, That true limes, grown in the production area, which fail to meet the requirements of such grade may be handled within the production, if such limes meet all other applicable requirements of this section and the minimum juice content requirement prescribed in the U.S. Standards for Persian (Tahiti) Limes, and are handled in containers other than the containers prescribed in 911.329 for the handling of limes between the production area and any point outside thereof;...[9]

Fifth, a system of laws that contains laws contradicting one another is inadequate because a situation covered by the contradictory laws requires the impossible. Individual laws are usually not self-contradictory. Instances of contradiction cited by business people result from contradictory rules issued by independent agencies responsible for the same area, or from contradictory rules issued by independent agencies on separate matters but when applied in a specific case lead to contradiction.

To illustrate just how complex the issue of the contradictory nature of law can become, consider, for example, a Sears suit against a number of federal agencies or officers, including the attorney general, the secretary of labor, the chairman of the Equal Opportunity Commission (EOC), and seven other cabinet officers and federal agencies. The issue of contention was the antidiscrimination statutes. Employers like Sears are not to discriminate on the basis of race, sex, age, or physical and mental handicaps. Yet the employer is required to give preference to veterans. But since veterans are overwhelmingly male, the required preference for veterans is in contradiction with the requirement that no preference be given to sex. Preferences for veterans ipso facto give preference to males. Moreover, other government programs, themselves discriminatory, make private-sector nondiscriminations more difficult to achieve. For example, Sears contends that the social security system has operated in a way to keep females out of the work force and hence that government quotas to hire given percentages of women are in conflict with the laws of the social security system. It is reported that

> The Company [Sears] asked the court to grant an injunction requiring the defendants "to coordinate the employment of anti-discrimination statutes" and to issue uniform guidelines that would tell employers "how to resolve existing conflicts between affirmative-action requirements based on race and sex and those based on veterans' status, age, and physical or mental handicaps."[10]

Without judging either Sears' motives for the suit or its behavior with respect to nondiscrimination, Sears' request for consistency is warranted in point of logic and good law.

Sixth, laws requiring what is impossible violate the fundamental purpose of law—the guidance of human conduct. This point seems so obvious that it hardly needs comment. Yet a tradition is growing in legal circles that clearly violates this principle. Strict liability holds a person or corporation liable for an act even when they are not responsible for it. Fuller points out the absurdity of allowing strict liability to expand so that it covers all activities.

> If strict liability were to attend, not certain specified forms of activity, but all activities, the conception of a causal connection between the act and the resulting injury would be lost. A poet writes a sad poem. A rejected lover reads it and is so depressed that he commits suicide. Who "caused" the loss of his life? Was it the poet, or the lady who jilted the deceased, or perhaps the teacher who aroused his interest in poetry? A man in a drunken rage shoots his wife. Who among those concerned with this event share the responsibility for its occurrence—the killer himself, the man who lent the gun to him, the liquor dealer who provided the gin, or was it perhaps the friend who dissuaded him from securing a divorce that would have ended an unhappy alliance?[11]

To conform to this requirement of good law, government regulations of business must rest on an adequate theory that delineates a class of undesirable acts that can result from business activity and then assess the extent to which business must be shown to be responsible for its acts before being held liable. It may well be, for example, that some activities (blasting) are so dangerous that strict liability should be invoked to discourage the activity in question. However, in many cases, strict liability is not the appropriate legal category and business people are quite right in being concerned about its ever-growing application.

Another condition that seems constantly violated in the government regulation of business is Fuller's seventh requirement of constancy through time. Government regulations are in a constant state of flux. One political party replaces another in the White House and the rules of the game change. Let there be a change in the leadership of a major congressional committee and rules change again.

Finally, there should be agreement between the law and the way it is administered. It is one thing to discover what the law is, but it is quite another to have the law enforced as written or enforced at all. Business people argue that federal and state regulatory bureaucracies are filled with petty individuals whose only means of gaining self-respect is by blocking the legitimate plans or aims of business. The time and effort involved in fighting these people discourages the growth of small business and encourages large businesses to provide either a psychic or monetary bribe to clear the roadblocks. There has been much talk about protecting employee rights within the firm. Devices must also be found to protect the legitimate interests of individual business from government bureaucracy.

To balance this criticism, the reader should know that Fuller's eight conditions for good law represent an ideal for a legal system. No legal system can conform completely to Fuller's ideals. Take the condition that the law must be stable through time. Change, including change in the conditions that produced the law in the first place, requires alterations in the law as well. Before OPEC and the oil crisis, cleaning up the atmosphere required regulations that discouraged the burning of coal. The oil embargo of the 1970s changed all that. Strategic considerations required encouragement for the use of coal. This shift in policy was expensive, but, given the changes in the world situation, the shift was necessary.

Fuller would agree here. Indeed, that is why he refers to his eight conditions as constituting a morality of the ideal rather than a morality of duty. However, Fuller is right in indicating that departures from these eight conditions do have costs, including the cost of undermining the law itself.

The reader should also realize that Fuller's ideal works best for statutes; it works somewhat less well for administrative decisions. For example, some might argue that regulatory law is something of a misnomer. Regulatory "law" has less in common with law than it does with judicial decisions or executive decisions. What constitutes the "disanalogy," Fuller's critics believe, is that judicial decisions or executive decisions are geared to specific situations and hence have less of the characteristic of generality than do statutes. Fuller might concede much of this point yet insist, correctly we believe, that his eight conditions still serve as an ideal for judicial and executive decisions as well. After all, Supreme Court rulings are viewed by everyone as establishing precedents. Perhaps the rule for the pricing of gas at the pumps need not be clear to everyone, but it should at least be clear to the oil companies, shouldn't it?

With these cautions in mind, Fuller's eight conditions for good law are fundamentally sound. Even when Fuller's eight conditions are recognized as an ideal, the fact that so much government regulatory policy stands in violation of them points out a serious inadequacy in the use of government regulation for achieving ethical corporate behavior. After all, government through its judicial system and through some regulation is, as we have seen, a requirement for a stable business environment. Both the law and business are rule-governed activities. When the rules that apply to business or that sustain and protect business violate the conditions for good law, business is harmed. Laws that are not stable adversely affect incentives and efficiency. Laws that are not clear or that require the impossible, or that apply retroactively, or that are contradictory, are unreasonable and unworkable. Both the business community and the public at large have every right to insist that laws regulating business should conform to the criteria for good law. However, even if government regulation generally conformed to Fuller's ideal, we should be wary of it, for fear of the law cannot be the sole motivator of ethical business practices.

In his excellent book, *Where the Law Ends*, Christopher Stone shows that the nature of law itself prevents it from being the sole condition for achieving corporate responsibility. Most business people have already moved beyond the point at which they believe the law is the final word in setting standards of corporate ethics. The view "If it's legal, it's okay" is not the prevailing notion in most corporations.

Nonetheless, the first response of the public, whenever it is unhappy, is to argue for the passage of new laws. If Stone's analysis is correct, this constant attempt to regulate corporate conduct through law is doomed to failure. First, there is the time-lag problem. Laws are passed only after the damage has been done, and often the damage is severe. What is needed is some way of preventing the damage in the first place. We cannot look to the law for that.

Second, there are limitations connected with the making of law. Stone observes that corporations play a very large role in formulating the law that governs them. Stone is not saying that corporations engage in bribery or intimidation to attain such influence; rather, Stone's point is that there is a natural corporate influence on the lawmaking process. After all, who has the expertise to know what regulations are reasonable? Is it not the corporations themselves? This expertise is usually a function of being in possession of relevant data that others cannot obtain—or at least cannot obtain without unwarranted difficulty. As Stone observes,

> The companies most closely associated with the problems may not know the answers either, but they certainly have the more ready access to the most probative information. It is their doctors who treat the employees' injuries; it is their chemists who live with and test the new compounds; it is their health records that gather absentee data.[12]

If the commonly held view that regulatory boards have as their members representatives of the industry being regulated is correct, such a phenomenon has a readily understandable explanation.

But corporate influence over laws regulating business is not the only inherent difficulty that stands in the way of implementing the law. Most decisions of public policy are inordinately complex. Consider nuclear power in the era of the energy crisis. It is clear that the waste-disposal problem has never been addressed satisfactorily and that the accident at the Three Mile Island facility near Harrisburg, Pennsylvania, raises serious questions about plant safety. Nonetheless, electrical energy is heavily dependent on oil, coal is a serious air pollutant, and the widespread use of solar power is not immediately technically or economically feasible. Given this dismal range of alternatives, how stringent should the regulation of nuclear power plants be? There simply is no consensus on the value issues in such a decision. As a society, we cannot agree on how the various issues are to be weighted. Without a majority consensus on the value issues, regulations that will be stable and enforceable are extremely hard to provide.

Another difficulty of government regulation concerns the assignment of responsibility—of tracing the line of causal connections so that we can determine who has been injured and who has perpetrated the injury. The adversary model of law presupposes the ability of a judge or jury to make that kind of determination. Most issues of corporate responsibility do not easily fit into that model. As Stone notes,

> The food we will eat tonight (grown, handled, packaged, distributed by various corporations) may contain chemicals that are killing us, or at least reducing our life expectancy, considerably. But (a) we cannot know with certainty the fact that we are being injured by any particular product; (b) it is difficult determining who might be injuring us—that is, even if we know that our bodies

are suffering a build-up of mercury, we are faced with an awesome task of pinning responsibility on any particular source of mercury; (c) we would have a difficult time proving the extent of our injuries....[13]

What such an example shows is that in many cases we cannot have much confidence in our ability to trace out the causal connections. Causal analysis works best in those cases where it is relatively easy to talk of the cause of some specific event. As you move away from that paradigm, causal analysis becomes less effective.

Still another difficulty of government regulation concerns problems with vagueness. When society attempts to draft laws to apply in situations in which there is no consensus on what ought to be done and in which it is difficult to determine causes and effects, the vagueness problem is much more serious. Harried lawmakers are forced to use broad, general terminology. Because the law cannot be directed to a specific cause and a specific effect, useless generality is to be expected. Besides, legislators must satisfy the demands of those who "want something done" yet at the same time draft laws that could receive a majority vote. Platitudinous generalities are ideal in such a situation.

However, the legislative compromise soon becomes the administrator's nightmare. These vague laws must be fleshed out with regulations. But regulations that evolve from the idiosyncratic views of individual bureaucrats rather than from a background of legislative intent are often cumbersome, inconsistent, and trivial. Many corporations that try to abide by such regulations feel harassed. Corporations cited as being in violation of the regulations feel unjustifiably singled out for punishment. As a result, the entire climate becomes poisoned and the broader and more important moral questions are lost in the daily battles between the government and the corporation.

Finally, laws have costly side effects. Consider the issue of drug safety laws. The stricter the controls, the greater the public's protections against injury from harmful drugs. But the stricter the controls, the longer the time lag between the discovery of a drug and its availability to the general public. In the time lag, people suffer and often die because that drug is not available. A possible example of inappropriate legislation is the so-called Delaney clause to the 1958 Food Additives Amendment to the Federal Food, Drug, and Cosmetic Act. That clause bans any food or drug that has been shown to cause cancer in laboratory animals. Yet artificial sweeteners are essential to the fight against diabetes and obesity. In a society where artificial sweeteners are banned, the deaths from the effects of diabetes are likely to exceed the deaths from cancer. Is not the goal of zero cancer deaths an unreasonable ideal? The law must set minimum standards, but it is not an effective vehicle for achieving ideals.

There are other costs, not mentioned by Stone, associated with government regulation. Some have argued that there is a substantial bias on the part of regulatory personnel to keep finding things wrong so that they would have something to regulate. After all, they are rewarded and promoted for doing something for their pay. Police officers are expected to make a certain number of arrests. Agents at the Internal Revenue Service are supposed to uncover a certain amount of income tax fraud. Anecdotes like the following abound. A company expects a visit from Occupational Safety and Health (OSHA) officials. Although the company has been most scrupulous in following OSHA rules, it realizes the OSH officials cannot leave the plant empty-handed, without citing some violations. Hence, company officials create a few easily fixable minor violations so that the OSH officials have something to cite. After the OSH officials leave, the violations are removed. Our point here is that the career interests of the regulators create pressures for overregulation.

On the basis of these arguments, the case is made that there are features of law that make it an inappropriate vehicle as an exclusive instrument of state policy for achieving the good society. This concludes our discussion of the strengths and weaknesses of self-regulation and government regulation as basic techniques for establishing a corporate milieu that will allow the individual business person and the individual business to act in a way favorably disposed to being ethical. Neither is sufficient by itself. The proper mixture of the two should be the ideal at which we aim.

WHY SHOULD BUSINESS BE MORAL?

But this leaves one question to be resolved. Even if there is agreement on society's, government's, and industry's part to be moral, why shouldn't the individual manager or business free-ride if at all possible?

The most popular answer to this question seems fairly straightforward. Nowadays it is quite common to assert that "It pays to be moral" or "Good ethics is good business." Indeed, the blurb on the cover of the recent book *Beyond the Bottom Line* by Tad Tuleja reads "How America's top corporations are proving that sound business ethics means good business practices." The argument is simply that the corporation should be moral because acting morally is in the interests of the corporation. Moral behavior, however, on the part of the corporation in such circumstances is simply rationally prudent behavior. In the literature of corporate ethics, many articles can be found that read like the admonitions of Epicurus against some of the less restrained hedonists. For example, Aristippus the Cyrenaic advocated the pursuit of pleasure, now, with as much intensity as possible. But Epicurus knew that tonight's party was followed by tomorrow's headache; hence, that restrained hedonism required only a bit of cheese for sumptuous dining. To draw an analogy, many corporate executives have lectured their counterparts on the virtues of deferred profit gratification. Low salaries and inadequate working conditions cut productivity. Ugly factories and an attitude of indifference toward the community in which one's plants are located generate hostility and a government climate not hospitable to business. Shoddy products ultimately drive the consumer away. In other words, the pursuit of the quick buck is not in the long-run interest of the firm. Because stable corporations need to be successful for the long term, "Look to long-run profits" is the official position of most corporate executives.

One situation deserves special comment, however. Some firms usually owned and operated by a few individuals have no interest in the long term. They can cheerfully quote John Maynard Keynes, "In the long run we are all dead." A firm specializing in souvenirs touting 1988 presidential candidate Richard Gephardt would have been mistaken in taking the long-run point of view. Many examples abound of enterprises where on rational self-interest grounds only the short run should be considered. Tonight's party is not followed by tomorrow's headache but by another party. Businesses in the entertainment industry, records, television, books, movies, nightclubs, toys, and games thrive on quick changes in tastes and fashion. The successful company gets on the pop-culture merry-go-round early and gets off early. What do you do with a million hula hoops when the craze has passed by? The clothing industry and the securities industry must also pay considerable attention to the short run. Simply put, corporations, like people, know that the deferring of pleasure or greater profit is not always rational. Indeed, many industries thrive on being successful in the short run. They either intend to make a sufficient killing so that the long run is provided for or to shift quickly from one short-term venture to another. Some businesses that thrive on maximizing in the short term are referred to both within and without the business community as fly-by-night operators. It is interesting to note that the response of "respectable" business executives to fly-by-nighters is not unlike that of "respectable" citizens to the excessively hedonistic or improvident members of the general community. There is something immoral about such behavior. What is needed, the corporations add, is something akin to the combination of law and morals that operates in the general society. Hence, respectable companies impress on the minds of their stockholders and the consuming public that their products are not shoddy, that their workers are not underpaid, and that they are taking positive steps to help solve society's problems. At the same time, Better Business Bureaus are created and responsible government regulations are endorsed.

Yet why should the fly-by-nighters pay any heed to their more "respectable" colleagues? For these companies, the demands of morality (socially responsible behavior) clash with the demands of self-interest (prudence). In such cases of genuine conflict, why should these companies be moral? Moreover, why should companies that consumer demand forces to focus on the short run be concerned with long-run morality?

An even more difficult question can be raised. An individual corporation may concede that morality (socially responsible behavior) is in the interests of the business community as a whole. However, what if the best interests of that corporation are achieved when the corporation pretends to be moral, and yet at the same time "cheats" whenever the manager thinks that he or she can get away with it. Success in that game will maximize the long-term interests of one's corporation. Kenneth Arrow puts it this way:

> After all an ethical code, however much it may be in the interest of all, is...not in the interest of any one firm. The code may be of value to the running of the system as a whole, it may be of value to all firms if all firms maintain it, and yet it will be to the advantage of any one firm to cheat, in fact the more so, the more other firms are sticking to it.[14]

It is here that the clash between morality and self-interest is unambiguous. The attempt to reconcile the two is impossible. What can now be said on behalf of an affirmative business response to the question "Why be moral?"

The main step in providing an answer to the question "Why be moral?" is to remember that business rests on contractual bases. The operation of a business, particularly when the business is a corporation, is not a matter of right. Robert A. Dahl has put the point this way:

> Today it is absurd to regard the corporation simply as an enterprise established for the sole purpose of allowing profit making. We the citizens give them special rights, powers, and privileges, protection, and benefits on the understanding that their activities will fulfill purposes. Corporations exist only as they continue to benefit us....Every corporation should be thought of as a social enterprise whose existence and decisions can be justified only insofar as they serve public or social purposes.[15]

Actually, Dahl's point not only indicates that the relation between business and society is contractual but it also spells out the nature of that contract. The corporation must not only benefit those who create it; it must benefit those who permit it (namely, society as a whole).

Naturally, an individual corporation could still ask why *it* should keep its agreements if it can get away with breaking or evading them. After all, in a competitive situation, one ought to take advantage of opportunities, and the opportunity to avoid or break the rules successfully is just another "lucky break" that should be capitalized upon. Of course, such opportunities will not occur very often; usually it is in the long-term interest of the firm to play by the rules (be moral). However, when long-term interest clashes with morality, a corporation would be foolish to sacrifice its interests to morality, wouldn't it?

What can be said on the other side? Arguments from Chapter 3 have already shown that the success of the corporate enterprise itself depends on parties' keeping their agreements. The survival of the very corporation contemplating a violation of the rules depends on the general practice of other corporations keeping their promises (contracts). If a corporation concedes this point, as we think it must, the question arises: On what grounds could it expect others to keep their agreements while it reneges on its? There are no grounds. Suppose the corporation insists that since it can depend on the others' good will to keep their word, it might as well take advantage of them. If a corporation publicly declared such a *free-rider* stance, it would be ostracized.

Now our potentially wayward corporation might respond that it is unique in some respect and hence immune from the general moral injunction to keep agreements. But how would such a uniqueness claim be justified? The other parties would have to accept it. Such an exemption would almost certainly not be granted. Indeed, the decision of the corporation to break the rules secretly gives prima facie warrant to the claim that the corporation knows it could not publicly plead for an exception. Hence, a corporation that requires the general practice of rule keeping but that contemplates violating the rules when it is to its advantage to do so is being inconsistent. It accepts the necessity of keeping contracts and yet seeks to violate such a contract. It seeks to make an exception of itself without being willing to allow other competing corporations to do the same thing in similar circumstances. Surely that is inconsistent. And this type of inconsistency, when practiced, is what we mean by unfair. Benefiting from rules that one publicly advocates but disobeys secretly is a paradigm case of acting hypocritically, dishonestly, and unfairly.

But suppose that our potentially wayward corporation is willing to subscribe to the following rule: "Corporations should keep their contracts unless they can successfully break or avoid them." Willingness to adopt this rule would avoid the charges of inconsistency. What would a business world that adopted that rule be like? Such a world would be essentially unstable. Relations among corporations and relations between corporations and their customers would resemble relations among suspicious and unfriendly nation-states. The world of business would resemble the world of hostile international relations, and surely that kind of instability is not advantageous to good business. So what answers can we give to the question "Why should a corporation be moral?"

1. Because usually it is in its interest (prudence).
2. Because morality is in the interest of the corporate community in general.
3. Because each individual corporation agreed to behave morally.
4. Because to renege on its agreement and yet expect others to keep theirs is unfair.
5. Because to agree to a set of rules to govern behavior and then to violate those rules secretly is inconsistent.
6. Because to agree to a condition where business and business persons may break the rules if they can get away with it is to undermine the environment necessary for business.

Finally, apart from the first reason, the real cynic can ask, "Why should I worry about the corporate community in general? I am out to beat the competition. Why worry about behaving morally or being unfair or inconsistent or undermining the environment necessary for business?" In the end there is no answer to give such a person. But consider such a cynic. He would be what Aristotle called the "unjust" man, where injustice is a deficiency in the fellow feeling necessary for a moral community to exist in the first place. Cynics often ridicule "bleeding hearts" but what is behind morality and ethics when all is said and done is caring. If one does not care for others, if one cannot put oneself in the other's place, one is, according to Aristotle either a god or a beast. If one lacks a caring attitude because the environment one grew up in made the person uncaring, then the environment is dehumanizing. Being human is being social, dependent, loving, and caring. There is no true human fulfillment and hence no ethics without these social virtues. Thus, to one who does not care, no satisfactory answer to the question "Why be moral?" exists. One who does care will concern oneself with justice and fairness and with creating an environment that makes those things possible.

This last point represents the final argument against those like Albert Carr who argue essentially that business should put prudence ahead of morality when it can get away with it. It may be that some readers have been persuaded by the main theme of this book. Certain moral standards do underlie business practices, and individual businesses and business people should adhere to those standards. However, whatever may be correct philosophically, the real world in which business must operate is characterized by some businesses breaking the rules when they can get away with it just as it is characterized by people being unethical when they can get away with it. To operate on a high moral plane in the "real" world is to put one's company at a disadvantage and hence to act "irresponsibly" in terms of profit maximization, just as to be just often puts oneself at a disadvantage. But as Aristotle observed centuries ago, it is not easy to be virtuous. Otherwise we would not praise it.

CONCLUSION

As philosophers, the authors of this book have an impression but are in no definitive position to make an accurate judgment on how extensive unethical business practices are. Not many people can. However, our experiences tell us that the great majority of businesses and business people operate at a fairly high level of ethical behavior. It is our best judgment that, when corporations or business persons begin to take moral shortcuts, either the government steps in and further constrains business or a Hobbesian state of nature develops in which each business ends up trying to cut the throat of its competitors. Either result undermines *the conditions of capitalism.*

Finally, many have argued that capitalism contains within itself the seeds of its own destruction. Karl Marx and Joseph Schumpeter are two of the most prominent examples. This book attests to the fact that we think the capitalist system can either be responsive to ethical demands, or reformed so that it becomes responsive. But, if not, consider a final twist to the "seeds of its own destruction" theme. To the extent that corporations undermine the ethical foundation that makes capitalism possible, they engage in behavior that will bring about their own destruction. We do not know how far current business practices depart from this ethical foundation. But we are convinced that business ethics is not the mere plaything of the public-relations office. Rather, business ethics as characterized in this book is absolutely necessary for business's continued existence. If business as we know it is to survive, there must be limits placed on the pursuit of profit.

NOTES

[1]W. Harvey Hegarty and Henry P. Sims, Jr., "Some Determinants of Unethical Decision Behavior: An Experiment," *Journal of Applied Psychology* 63(4) (August 1978), pp. 451–457 and W. Harvey Hegarty and Henry P. Sims, Jr., "Organizational Philosophy, Policies and

Objectives Related to Unethical Decision Behavior: A Laboratory Experiment," *Journal of Applied Psychology* 64(3) (June 1979), pp. 331–338.

[2]Ivan Hill (ed.), *The Ethical Basis of Economic Freedom* (Chapel Hill, N.C.: American Viewpoint Inc., 1976), p. 292.

[3]H.L.A. Hart, *The Concept of Law* (New York: Oxford University Press, 1961), 124–41.

[4]Theodore Purcell, "Electing an Angel's Advocate to the Board," *Management Review*, 65 (May 1976):9–10.

[5]Christopher D. Stone, "Controlling Corporate Misconduct," *The Public Interest*, 48, (Summer 1977):67.

[6]Thomas C. Schelling, "Command and Control," in Thomas L. Beauchamp and Norman E. Bowie, *Ethical Theory and Business*, 1st ed. (Englewood Cliffs, N.J.: Prentice-Hall, 1979), 218.

[7]Lon Fuller, *The Morality of Law*, rev. ed. (New Haven, Conn.: Yale University Press, 1964), 39.

[8]Ibid., 46.

[9]*Federal Register*, 44, (68), April 6, 1979.

[10]"Sears Turns the Tables," *Newsweek*, February 5, 1979, pp. 87–89.

[11]Fuller, *Morality of Law*, p. 76.

[12]C.D. Stone, *Where the Law Ends* (New York: Harper & Row, Publishers, 1975), 96.

[13]Ibid., 104.

[14]Kenneth Arrow, "Social Responsibility and Economic Efficiency," *Public Policy*, 21 (Summer 1973):315.

[15]Robert A. Dahl, "A Prelude to Corporate Reform," in *Corporate Social Policy*, Robert L. Heilbroner and Paul London, eds. (Reading, Mass.: Addison-Wesley Publishing Company, 1975), 18–19.

Index